HEARTSPRING PUBL

HEBREWS

THE 3:16 SERIES

STRENGTH
FOR THE
JOURNEY

JEFF SNELL

HEARTSPRING PUBLISHING · JOPLIN, MISSOURI

Copyright © 2003
HeartSpring Publishing
www.heartspringpublishing.com
A division of College Press Publishing Co.

Toll-free order line 800-289-3300
On the web at www.collegepress.com

The 3:16 Series (Colossians 3:16)
"Let the word of Christ dwell in you richly . . . ."

Cover design by Brett Lyerla
Interior design by Dan Rees

Library of Congress Cataloging-in-Publication Data

Snell, Jeff, 1966–
   Strength for the journey / by Jeff Snell.
       p. cm. — (The 3:16 series)
   ISBN 0-89900-917-4 (pbk.)
  1. Bible. N.T. Hebrews—Textbooks. I. Title. II. Series.
  BS2775.55.S65 2003
  227'.87'0071—dc22

                             2003017848

HEARTSPRING'S 3:16 SERIES

The Apostle Paul encouraged Christians in the first century and therefore us today to "**allow the Word of Christ to dwell in us richly**" (Colossians 3:16, *NIV*).

The 3:16 Series is based on this verse in Colossians. The series is designed primarily for small group study and interaction but will also prove fruitful for individual study. Each participant is encouraged to read the chapter before the group's meeting. The interaction questions are designed to be the focal point of your group's discussion time.

Psalm 119:11 says, "*I have hidden Your Word in my heart that I might not sin against You.*" One noteworthy feature of this series is that each study includes a suggested memory verse (a short verse or two from the passage that is being studied). A 5×8-inch card has been inserted at the back of the book for you to take these verses with you wherever you go and refer to them throughout your day.

The HeartSpring Publishing website will continually be updated with small group ideas and tips to further enhance your study of each New Testament book in the 3:16 series. Be sure to log on to www.heartspringpublishing.com (College Press) frequently!

"Let the Word of Christ . . . have the run of the house.
Give it plenty of room in your lives."
(Col. 3:16 *The Message*)

PREVIEWING OUR STUDY OF HEBREWS

JEFF SNELL

Chapter One: Guidance for the Journey (Hebrews 1:1-4)

This chapter introduces our study by focusing on Jesus as the supreme means of God's self-revelation and, therefore, our reliable guide on the journey through this life. We'll begin with a story of a time when my family was lost on a journey and we lacked a reliable guide. We'll then work through the first four verses of the letter, which function as an overture introducing the major themes in Hebrews. This chapter contrasts Jesus with other spiritual guides and points toward the confidence that comes from having a *sure* guide.

Chapter Two: Perspective for the Journey (Hebrews 1:5-14)

This chapter focuses on the rest of Hebrews 1 in order to paint a portrait of the divine nature of Jesus Christ. Seeing the majesty of Christ enables us to journey through life with a greater sense of perspective, because we see both him and ourselves in a clearer light. The chapter begins with a story from the popular children's series, *The Chronicles of Narnia*. This story illustrates the principle that as the Christian matures, he/she recognizes God and the inherent majesty of God to a greater extent. We'll then see how each of the Old Testament passages quoted in Hebrews 1 demonstrates the majesty/deity of Christ.

Chapter Three: A Leader for the Journey (Hebrews 2:1–3:6)

While chapter two addresses the fact that Jesus was in fact fully God, this chapter addresses the full *humanity* of Jesus. We'll focus in this study on Jesus as our "trailblazer." That is to say, Jesus is the one who has blazed the trail from us to the Father, so that we can follow his lead. He blazed the trail by becoming a man—which is typically described as "the incarnation." Our study will focus on the *appropriateness* of the incarnation, the *necessity* of the incarnation and the *results* of the incarnation. We will also address the contrast between Jesus and Moses in Hebrews 3. Both were faithful leaders, but Jesus is preeminent because he is God's Son.

Chapter Four: Peace for the Journey (Hebrews 3:1–4:13)

This chapter focuses on the Sabbath rest concept in Hebrews. We'll explore the analogy between these Hebrew Christians and the initial Israelite generation in Canaan. "Rest" in this passage is defined as a spiritual state of well being that results from a right relationship with God. We'll focus on both the present and the future components of this rest. We'll also learn that the Bible's goal in portraying the future is to motivate faithfulness in the present. A part of the imagery in this section involves the idea of being on a journey toward home, and how a clear picture of home enables people to persevere on a difficult journey.

Chapter Five: Warnings for the Journey (Hebrews 5:11–6:20)

This chapter will focus on the famous *warning* section of the book of Hebrews by considering it within the overall exhortation section in which it is found. The challenge is to avoid placing ourselves in positions of spiritual vulnerability. The recipients of this letter were considering a conscious decision to revert from Christianity back to Judaism. Therefore, their status is different than many of those we think of when trying to apply this passage. The passage also acknowledges that spiritual laziness can cause one to passively drift into a position of great vulnerability. We will be challenged not to grow lax on the journey due to either the difficulty of the journey or the length of the journey.

Chapter Six: A Bridge for the Journey (Hebrews 5:1-10; 7:1-28)

These are the sections of Hebrews that deal most specifically with the high priesthood of Jesus. Built into the imagery of priesthood is the idea of being a bridge builder. In Jesus' case, he was both the builder of the bridge and the bridge. This section will deal with the reasons why Jesus' high priesthood was superior to the levitical priesthood, but will primarily do so with a view to how these differences are significant for us. Jesus' priesthood is enduring because it is apart from genealogy, based on the power of an indestructible life, guaranteed by an oath from God, etc. The enduring nature of this bridge will especially be addressed.

Chapter Seven: Privileges for the Journey (Hebrews 8:1-13)

This chapter addresses the new covenant prophecy from Jeremiah 31. It addresses the differences between the old covenant and the new covenant as established in this passage. Included are the differences between external and internal realities and the difference between temporary and final forgiveness from sin. The journey motif is integrated into this section through the idea that the journey is a *relationship* (thus the emphasis in the covenant language of the chapter).

Chapter Eight: Cleansing for the Journey (Hebrews 9:1–10:18)

This chapter addresses freedom from sin and the guilt which is a byproduct of sin. This chapter will incorporate the journey motif through a Bunyanlike portrait of the difference between going through life loaded down by a heavy burden and a journey through life once freed of the burden. The chapter emphasizes some of the central teachings of this section: that Jesus' sacrifice involves superior blood, that it is presented in a superior location, and that it is a once-for-all sacrifice.

Chapter Nine: Checkpoints on the Journey (Hebrews 10:19-25)

This chapter is based on a brief paragraph that is structurally significant in the book of Hebrews. It functions as a hinge passage that summarizes the entire preceding portion of the letter and introduces the remaining material. There are three significant commands in this section: the command to draw near to God, the command to hold unswervingly to faith, and the command to spur one another along (by not forsaking assembly). At this stage in our journey through the book of Hebrews, it is helpful to pause and consider some of what we have seen thus far and to share regarding the progress that is being made.

Chapter Ten: Confidence for the Journey (Hebrews 11:1-40)

This chapter deals specifically with the example of Abraham as representative of the entire chapter (although relatively brief reference will be made to the whole chapter). It deals with the challenges to Abraham's faith, and how Abraham evidenced authentic faith through his journey. The chapter addresses faith even when we don't know where we are going, faith even when God's promise seems too good to be true, and faith even when God's voice seems to be confusing. The journey motif is built in throughout, but especially regarding the powerful motivation that comes from knowing that others have made the journey before us.

Chapter Eleven: Resolve for the Journey (Hebrews 12:1-13)

This chapter deals with the importance of viewing times of difficulty and persecution as a means God uses in order to fashion us into his likeness. The example of Jesus (vv. 1-3) and the Proverbs 3 passage both teach us that we need to view our suffering for Christ as something God is big enough to use in ways that are in accordance with his ultimate purposes. Difficulty on a journey can increase one's emotional resolve and physical strength. Similarly, the experience of persecution can actually serve to spiritually strengthen the believer who is willing to fully partner with God on the journey.

Chapter Twelve: Reminders for the Journey (Hebrews 13:1-25)

This chapter contains several reminders, all of which relate to community life. We are not taking this journey alone, but in community. The challenges of the journey provide opportunities for community to be fragmented, but they are also opportunities for a sense of community to be fostered. These opportunities are embraced as we protect our marriages, guard against greed, function as effective leaders/followers, and care for the Christian persecuted. The challenges of the journey, the beauty of the journey and the importance of the journey demand that we express concern for the well-being of others as well as ourselves.

TABLE OF CONTENTS

STRENGTH FOR THE JOURNEY

CHAPTER ONE

GUIDANCE FOR THE JOURNEY

HEBREWS 1:1-4

Several summers ago, our family vacation included a journey that took us up the western coast of Michigan, across central Michigan into Ontario, and then back into southeastern Michigan. We crossed the United States/Canadian border at the point where Windsor, Ontario, meets Detroit. It seemed like a good idea at the time. We were not familiar with Detroit and thought it would be an interesting and convenient place to reenter the States. It did turn out to be interesting. Convenient it was not, for we encountered three significant problems. First, that particular border crossing handles more city traffic than any other one separating the aforementioned countries. Second, the Michigan 500 (a NASCAR race) was taking place southwest of Detroit the following day and there were an estimated additional one million people in the metro area that weekend. Third, major road renovations hampered the city that summer. Almost all access ramps to Interstate 94 were closed and we promptly missed the only one that was open from our direction. A further complication immediately surfaced, since traffic routing decisions made a return to that entrance impossible (or at least illegal).

At that moment, we desperately needed a guiding word. The Detroit map insert in our atlas was virtually worthless, because all the rules had changed. My wife was of no practical assistance. She had been ambushed by a stomach virus and sat immobilized in the passenger seat. Our three children possessed no helpful insights, since the oldest was five. (They each knew enough to remain quiet, however.) I stopped to seek the advice of a few locals. The best (and only printable) advice I received was "lots of luck." While we eventually made it home, the experience is etched into our family history. A journey without guidance can rapidly develop into a source of overwhelming frustration.

> A journey without guidance can rapidly develop into a source of overwhelming frustration.

Our vacation experience is descriptive of what some folks encounter in their journey through life. While God has woven into us a deep desire for himself, nothing is more frustrating than to have that deep longing for a divine destination without any hint of how to reach it. A fragment from an ancient prayer effectively captures this agony. Penned over 2500 years ago, it communicates with transparency emotions that span the centuries:

Oh god whom I know or do not know, my transgressions
    are many; great are my sins;
Oh goddess whom I know or do not know, my transgressions
    are many; great are my sins.

The transgression which I have committed, indeed I do not know.
The sin which I have done, indeed I do not know.
The forbidden thing which I have eaten, indeed I do not know;
The prohibited place on which I have set foot, indeed I do not know.

The lord in the anger of his heart looked at me; the god in the rage of
    his heart confronted me;
When the goddess was angry with me, she made me become ill.
The god whom I know or do not know has oppressed me;
The goddess whom I know or do not know has placed suffering upon
    me.

Although I am constantly looking for help, no one takes me by the hand;
When I weep they do not come to my side.
I utter laments, but no one hears me; I am troubled, I am
Overwhelmed; I cannot see . . .

I kiss the feet of my goddess; I crawl before thee.
How long, O my goddess, whom I know or do not know,
    until thy hostile heart will be quieted?

Man is dumb; he knows nothing;
Mankind, everyone that exists—what does he know?

Guidance for the Journey

Whether he is committing sin or doing good, he does not
even know.
O my lord, do not cast thy servant down; he is plunged
by the waters of a swamp; take him by the hand.
The sin which I have done, turn into goodness;
The transgression which I have committed, let the wind
carry away;
My many misdeeds strip off like a garment . . .
Remove my transgressions and I will sing thy praise.
May thy heart, like the heart of a real mother, be
quieted toward me;
Like a real mother and a real father may it be quieted
toward me.[1]

Sense this man's desperation. Share his bewilderment as he tries to understand the workings of supernatural power in his life and in his world. Agonize with him as he longs for some understanding of the boundaries that govern appropriate behavior. Feel his gnawing sense of guilt. Watch him grovel before a "supreme being" that is shrouded in total mystery and veiled by vagueness. Feel his pain. He is driven by the desire for meaning, order, understanding, and peace. Something in him wants to reach out to this supreme one; he longs for things to be made right. The silence of his god's response is deafening.

He is not alone, you know. The twentieth century was filled with the voices of those struggling against the seeming silence of God. Author Kent Hughes recounts an event from the life of well-known Swedish filmmaker Ingmar Bergman. While listening to classical music one day, Bergman had a sudden mental picture of a nineteenth-century cathedral. He imagined himself coming before a picture of Jesus and, in his dreamlike state, Bergman said to the picture, "Speak to me! I will not leave this cathedral until you speak to me!" The figure in the picture did not speak. What was Bergman's response? That same year he produced a film, *The Silence*, which presented characters who despair of ever finding God.[2] Like all good filmmakers, Bergman was not simply speaking for himself. He was representing an entire segment of twentieth-century western culture.

The opening words of Hebrews shatter both ancient
and contemporary notions of a God who is silent.

The opening words of Hebrews shatter both ancient and contemporary notions of a God who is silent. The very first phrase of this letter contrasts God with lifeless idols of ancient paganism and modern perceptions of his muteness. Although the first four verses of Hebrews 1 are a single sentence in the original language of the New Testament, the core of this initial statement is *GOD HAS SPOKEN!* The theme of a God who speaks brackets the entire Bible. Genesis 1:3 records God creating with a word, and a dominant refrain in the first chapter is, "And God said." The second-to-last verse of the Bible contains the risen Christ saying, "Yes, I am coming soon." Between these bookends are numerous references to the self-revealing activity of God through his words. The Old Testament Scriptures contain 3,808 occurrences of the phrases "The Lord said," "The Lord spoke," and "The word of the Lord came." Even this substantial figure barely scratches the surface of God's communication to people in the Old Testament.

The writer of Hebrews, however, makes it immediately clear that God's instruments of self-revelation are not equal in significance or impact. The text does so by establishing an immediate contrast between the multitude of ways God has revealed himself in the past and the one ultimate means through which he has made himself known. The contrasts become especially clear when visualized as follows:

In the past	BUT	in these last days
God spoke		he has spoken
to our forefathers		to us
through the prophets		in his Son
at many times/various ways		

The first contrast addresses the matter of WHEN. The era described as *past* is the era prior to the coming of Jesus. This becomes more evident when *past* is contrasted with *last days*. Overall New Testament usage of this term demonstrates that the phrase *last days* does not refer to a literal last few days; rather, it refers to the final era in God's covenant-making activity with people (Acts 2:16-17). The era referred to as *last days* was inaugurated at the first appearing of Jesus and concludes at the second coming of Jesus. For purposes of this contrast, the writer of Hebrews divides all of human history into two categories: the era before Jesus came to earth and the era once Jesus came to earth.

> The writer of Hebrews divides all of human history into two categories: the era before Jesus came to earth and the era once Jesus came to earth.

The second contrast involves the issue of TO WHOM. The term *forefathers*, in this passage, essentially indicates all people of faith who received communication from God prior to the coming of Jesus. The term *us*, therefore, does not only refer to the particular generation of

Christians receiving the material in Hebrews. It represents those living in the era designated as the last days.

The third contrast tackles the question of THROUGH WHOM. *Prophets* as used by the writer of Hebrews does not refer exclusively to the writing prophets of the Old Testament books that bear their names. It indicates all those through whom God worked in this first era to reveal himself to humanity. Collectively they are contrasted with the revealing activity of God achieved via his *Son*. The point is simply this: prophets were able to speak for God, but the Son was able to speak as God (as is more clearly seen in the phrases that follow this initial contrast).

> Prophets were able to speak for God,
> but the Son was able to speak as God

The final comparison evaluates the matter of HOW MANY WAYS. A contrast is established between the diverse and numerous ways God revealed himself in the previous era compared to the single supreme way he has revealed himself in the person of Jesus. Assessing the supremacy of God's self-revelation does not require counting the ways. It requires weighing the ways. God demonstrated his communicative creativity prior to the coming of Jesus. He employed speech, proverbs, prophecy, laws, dreams, visions, guidance through stones, testing, plagues, provisions, symbolic rituals and actions, furniture, and a talking donkey, just to name a few! All of these, however, paled in comparison to his ultimate means of communication—the presence of Jesus on earth.

The issues are crucial. They demonstrate that God is a communicator. He did not leave his people without a word in the past era. He transmitted truth with unsurpassed *variety* so they would have some understanding of his nature, will, and ways. This revelation was timely, helpful, and accurate. In the era inaugurated by his Son, however, he has revealed himself with unsurpassed *quality*. Like the people who originally received the book of Hebrews, we have not seen Jesus with our own eyes (Heb 2:3). Unlike them, we can read an accurate record from those who did. God is still speaking through his Word.

Next time you are tempted to think we serve a gagged God, remember one more thing. It was God who took the initiative in communicating with people in the first place. Human history is not the story of people reaching out to God, it is the story of God reaching out to people.

> Human history is not the story of people reaching out
> to God, it is the story of God reaching out to people.

I used to find myself thinking about God when I would play hide-and-seek with my kids. Have you played hide-and-seek with a youngster recently? It has to be one of the easiest games in the world, at least when you are the one doing the seeking. When playing with our kids, I would simply count to twenty and begin walking around the back yard. Like all parents seem to do, I would express high-decibel wonderment at their marvelous hiding ability. Though I pondered the possible hiding spots with exaggerated tones, I didn't exactly wear out my shoes playing the game. Why? Everyone who has ever played hide-and-seek with a child knows the answer. Before long, I would see a shrub growing an arm or a tree growing a leg. My kids, like most kids, didn't play hide-and-seek because they wanted to be hidden. They played for the joy of being found.

You know, God is a little like that. He delights in revealing something of himself to the crown jewel of his creation. If you are earnestly seeking after God, and you are willing to look around, the last thing you have to be concerned about is the possibility that God will hide himself from you. He has long since committed himself to revelation, and the desires of his heart have not changed.

As we begin this trip through Hebrews for the sake of gaining strength for our life journey, the impact of these few verses is profound. When many folks evaluate the success of a small group Bible study session, they begin by considering the extent to which people talked. Certainly such interaction is both valuable and desirable. It does, after all, take away from the community-building component of Bible study when no one speaks! The writer of Hebrews, however, would remind us of a profound irony: the first key to an effective group study is not getting people to talk—it is getting people to listen. In a room full of voices anxious to be heard, the most important one belongs to the Attendee who remains unseen. Though he may not need a spot in the living room, he will be most actively involved in the group. He will show up every week and will always have something important to say. Let's be sure to listen. It is pretty hard to follow guidance that you don't hear. 📖

[1] James Pritchard, ed., *Ancient Near Eastern Texts Relating to the Old Testament* (Princeton: Princeton University Press, 1969).

[2] Kent Hughes, *Hebrews: An Anchor for the Soul*, vol. 1 (Wheaton: Crossway Books, 1993), 22-23.

‡

C
H
A
P
T
E
R

1 *Guidance for the Journey*

Activities for Your Group's Journey

1. Spend some time praying (individually) before the group meeting. Reflect back on your past week or two and ask God to give you a hearing checkup. On a scale of 1-10, how successfully have you been listening to God? If you are comfortable doing so, share your current condition with the group.

2. Assess the reasons for your current hearing condition. If you have been doing well, what practices or processes in your life have contributed to this sensitivity toward God's voice? If you have been doing poorly, what practices or processes have blocked your hearing capacity?

3. Hebrews 1:1-4 emphasizes that God has ultimately revealed himself through Jesus. How do we encounter Jesus when he is not physically present among us? What are the ways in which we "hear" God speak? Which of these ways is the most important? Why?

4. Close the group session by praying specifically for everyone's hearing capacity to increase. Divide the group so that everyone is praying for someone else's hearing capacity during the time between meetings.

5. Assess your progress between meetings and be prepared to share if/how your hearing has improved when you meet again.

 Memory Verse Hebrews 1:1-2

In the past God spoke to our forefathers through the prophets at many times and in various ways, [2]but in these last days he has spoken to us by his Son, whom he appointed heir of all things, and through whom he made the universe.

CHAPTER TWO

PERSPECTIVE FOR THE JOURNEY

HEBREWS 1:5-14

Christians of all ages have enjoyed and benefited from The Chronicles of Narnia. Perhaps part of the appeal possessed by these seven children's books is due to their underlying travel theme. The four children who comprise the primary characters of the series experience a variety of adventuresome journeys that are all part of one larger journey.

On one such adventure, contained in the volume titled *Prince Caspian*, the children are transported from a railway station into the magical world that is Narnia. Beckoned unknowingly by a horn that magically functions as a distress signal, the children find themselves in a familiar world and yet an unfamiliar place. They set out to locate those in distress, accompanied by a dwarf sent to find them. As they begin to climb down a gorge, Lucy, the youngest, sees something the others cannot. The object of her gaze is Aslan, a lion designed by author C.S. Lewis to represent Christ. Her companions on the journey do not believe her report, and they all go to sleep. Lucy awakens in the middle of the night, however, and one of my favorite scenes in the entire Chronicles series unfolds.

A circle of grass, smooth as a lawn, met her eyes, with dark trees dancing all round it. And then—oh joy! For *He* was there: the huge Lion, shining white in the moonlight, with his huge black shadow underneath him. . . .

"Aslan, Aslan. Dear Aslan," sobbed Lucy. "At last." The great beast rolled over on his side so that Lucy fell, half sitting and half lying between his front paws. . . .

"Welcome, child," he said.

"Aslan," said Lucy, "you're bigger."

"That is because you are older, little one," answered he.

"Not because you are?"

"I am not. But every year you grow, you will find me bigger."[1]

"Every year you grow, you will find me bigger." These are promising, but challenging words. I suspect Lewis's intent in using the term "older" is to imply spiritual as well as biological advancement. When was the last time you measured your spiritual growth by this yardstick? When we think of progress in our spiritual journey, we tend to think in different categories: an increased awareness of grace, a growing desire for righteousness, an increased burden for the lost, more involvement in service opportunities or small groups. Such things are desirable, of course. Lewis reminds us, however, that one barometer of spiritual growth is a deepening awareness of the majesty of Christ.

> One barometer of spiritual growth is a deepening awareness of the majesty of Christ.

Like us, those who originally received the book of Hebrews needed a reminder in this area. As we saw in the previous lesson, Hebrews begins with a portrait of a God who reveals himself through Christ. The remainder of Hebrews 1 paints a majestic portrait of the One through whom God has revealed himself. The writer of this material accomplishes his goal by making seven significant statements about Jesus in Hebrews 1:2-4. He follows the seven statements with seven Old Testament passages that reinforce the truths and tone just established. Before we consider the specifics, it is important to understand why the writer of Hebrews is presenting this picture.

The Significance of Jesus' Supremacy

A glance at our passage immediately indicates that God is deeply concerned about our grasp of the relationship between Jesus and angels. The issue receives such detailed attention for three reasons.

First and foremost, he is trying to say that the new relationship available with God through Christ is superior to that available to people before the coming of Christ. At first glance, this may not seem to have anything to do with the superiority of Jesus over angels. Hebrews 2:1-4, an exhortation based on the message of chapter one, clarifies the issue. The relationship that existed between God and Israel (commonly called the old covenant) was initiated due to God's kindness, not

Israel's merit (Exod 19:4). Israel's part of the deal, however, was to keep over 600 regulations as a demonstration of allegiance to God. Moses received the old covenant requirements on Mount Sinai (Exod 24:18), but how did God communicate those laws to Moses? Deuteronomy 33:32, Hebrews 2:2-3, Acts 7:53, and Galatians 3:19 provide the answer. God gave the old covenant to Moses through angels. Hebrews 8:5 describes Jesus as the mediator of a new covenant. Hebrews is demonstrating that the new covenant is superior to the old, because a better mediator put it into effect. A superior mediator indicates a superior covenant agreement between God and people.

Second, Hebrews is going to develop a portrait of Jesus' high priestly ministry in our behalf. The writer is demonstrating that Jesus is fully God, and therefore fully able to represent God when functioning as our high priest. (This subject surfaces most completely in chapter six of our study, but it is a continuous theme throughout.) While angels come up in the discussion, the text is trying more than anything to say something about Jesus! Attempting to reduce him to the status of an angel contradicts the message of Hebrews 1.

Third, these Christians lived in a world that had gone angel crazy. Jewish and Christian speculation on the significance and work of angels saturated first-century writing and thinking. The emphasis on angels in Colossae had even resulted in some beginning to worship angels (Col 2:18). Some may have been tempted to reduce Jesus to the status of angels; others may have been tempted to elevate angels to the position of Jesus. Either way, the problem was the same. There is no direct evidence that the recipients of this letter were specifically struggling with angel worship, but it is clear they needed a biblical perspective on angels. The author of Hebrews is primarily demonstrating the supremacy of Christ, but in so doing he refutes those who would overly emphasize or elevate angelic beings.

Stating Jesus' Supremacy

The seven statements in Hebrews 1:1-4 present the book's overall message in embryonic form. Like an overture in a musical, these verses provide us with a brief synopsis of the plot in advance of its full development. Jesus is presented as equal in status with God prior to the incarnation, faithful to God through the incarnation, and vindicated by God as a result of the incarnation.

The Son is first described as *heir of all*. This statement is a natural byproduct of Jesus' sonship and anticipates what is said about him in the following statements. Because Jesus has created all, he is heir of all

(Col 1:16). Because he has redeemed us, he receives us as an inheritance (Eph 1:18). Everything that belongs to God belongs to Jesus.

He is *creator and sustainer* as well. God is described as creating in Genesis 1, but Hebrews 1 shows that when God created, he did so *through* Jesus (John 1:3; Col 1:16). What Jesus created, he is equally capable of sustaining (Col 1:17). Jesus keeps "natural law" functioning consistently. We can count on gravity to gravitate because of him!

The next two terms bridge the pre-incarnate Son and the fully human Jesus. He is described as the *perfect representation of the Father's identity*. Everything that makes God the Father deity, Jesus possesses. When Jesus is referred to as the "radiance" of God's glory, it refers to the tangible splendor that accompanies God's presence. Frequently, the glory of God is evidenced in the Old Testament through incredible brightness. On the Mount of Transfiguration (Mark 9:3), Jesus demonstrated what the Apostle Paul later discovered (Acts 9:3). Jesus is fully God, and therefore exudes the same glory characteristic of the Father. In exhibiting that glory on earth, Jesus was like the sun, which produces light, rather than the moon, which simply reflects it.

Next, Hebrews describes Jesus as *purifier of our sin*. This term draws heavily from the book of Leviticus and emphasizes an idea that receives its fullest development in chapters nine and ten. Jesus is the one sacrifice that can remove the guilt of sin.

Jesus is the one sacrifice that can remove the guilt of sin.

Finally, Jesus is presented as an *exalted ruler*, next to God the Father, at the place of highest status. Present with the Father, he is able to intercede directly in our behalf. Having completed the work of redemption, he is resurrected, exalted, and vindicated by the Father. One with the Father in essence, he is able to rule over all.

Showing Jesus' Supremacy

The best evidence the writer of Hebrews could give to support his seven statements was quotations from the Old Testament Scriptures. This was the Bible for early Christians; therefore, it was the way the author could show his audience "the Bible says so." These passages especially emphasize the concept of Jesus as a ruling figure. Several come from a category of Psalms known as royal Psalms. Israel used these songs in situations that related to the Jewish king, and Christians adopted them as a part of their working vocabulary when preaching and teaching about Jesus. The remaining Old Testament citations use royal images and language to describe Jesus in ways that connect him specifically with God's reign. The cumulative effect of these passages creates an atmosphere similar to that experienced by U.S. citizens when they hear a specific song—"Hail to the Chief."

The first two texts are linked by the common words "Son" and "Father." Psalm 2:7 functioned in Israel as a coronation hymn for a new king. It reflects the understanding within Israel (as well as other nations) that a ruling figure possessed a special relationship to God. God himself alluded to Psalm 2:7 at Jesus' baptism (Mark 1:11), and Paul specifically connected it to Jesus' resurrection (Acts 13:32-33). Second Samuel 7:14 records the promise from God to David that an enduring kingdom would come from his line of descendants. This promise was not initially fulfilled, since there was no descendent on the throne only a few generations after David's death. The New Testament indicates Jesus fulfilled this promise (Matt 1:1; Luke 1:32-33).

The next set of Scriptures contrasts the status of Jesus with that of angels. Hebrews portrays God speaking, as it were, the words of Deuteronomy 32:43 to the angels for us to overhear. They are commanded to worship Jesus, who is referred to in Hebrews 1:5 as the firstborn. This does not mean Jesus was the first one created; Hebrews 1 has already emphasized that he is creator not creation. "Firstborn" is a term of status that reflects Jesus' position as heir. (In the Old Testament the firstborn son was an heir in a special sense). The point here is that Jesus deserves worship and angels give it. This is natural since they are servants, which is the emphasis of Psalm 104:4. This Psalm especially describes God in relationship to the created order. It presents him as creator, sustainer, and provider. Just as Hebrews 1:3 attributes these characteristics to Jesus, Hebrews 1:7 takes a passage that originally applied to God the Father and says it applies to Jesus as well. The greatest distinction that exists is the one between creator and creation. Jesus is the former, not the latter.

"Firstborn" is a term of status
that reflects Jesus' position as heir.

The next passage is from Psalm 45, which was used at the wedding of a king. Terms like throne, scepter, anointing, and kingdom provide the royal overtones to this Old Testament song. Here, they show the duration of Jesus' reign (forever), the nature of his reign (righteous), and the tone of his reign (joyous). Furthermore, God is described as saying to Jesus, "Your throne, O God." It is as if the writer of Hebrews is saying, "What does it take to convince you that Jesus is fully God? Would the voice of God himself convince you? Here it is!" The enduring nature of Jesus' reign and his fundamental consistency are stressed through the quoting of Psalm 102:25-27. Dress socks that develop holes and carpet that fades are representative of the entire created order. In contrast to this stands the eternal, unchanging Lord of the Universe.

> "What does it take to convince you that Jesus is fully God?
> Would the voice of God himself convince you? Here it is!"

The chain of Scripture quotations concludes with Psalm 110:1, the most frequently cited Old Testament passage in the New Testament. It pictures the ultimate rulership of Jesus over all and his exaltation—a fact in the present, but tangibly experienced by all in the future. The image comes from victory celebrations during the Old Testament era. During a special ceremony, the vanquished king was brought before the victorious king. The defeated king would then lie on his back while the dominant king would place his foot at the throat of his victim. This symbolized the total defeat and complete humiliation of the king and his subjects. (The closest biblical parallel to this is found in Josh 10:24). No wonder this passage is employed so frequently in the New Testament as a way to describe the victory and vindication of Jesus!

Seeing Jesus' Supremacy

We desperately need to recapture the biblical portrait of the exalted Christ. Some misunderstand the identity of Jesus, viewing him as an angelic equivalent, a wise teacher, or a misguided revolutionary. Others understand the identity of Jesus correctly, but fail to acknowledge him as king. This portrait of Jesus should not merely cause us to scratch our heads in wonderment; it should cause us to fall to our knees in reverence. He deserves it.

Of course, we also need it. We cannot possibly view our journey from the proper perspective if we don't have Jesus in proper perspective. Our problems seem larger than life when we aren't accurately viewing the Lord of life. The lack of world peace is more overwhelming when we aren't focused on the Prince of Peace. Maybe what we need is less focus on ourselves and more focus on him. As the chorus "Turn Your Eyes upon Jesus" advises, we need to let everything else grow dim in comparison to the light of his glory. I don't know how much empty packing space you have available on this journey. If we want the trip to go well, however, we should probably find room for a songbook.

---

[1] C.S. Lewis, *Prince Caspian: The Return to Narnia* (New York: MacMillan Books, 1951), 135-136.

24

✝

C
H
A
P
T
E
R

2   *Perspective for the Journey*

Activities for Your Group's Journey

1. Reflect on the quote from Lewis's book. Are you growing in your awareness of the Christ's majesty? Pray for an increased awareness of His greatness in the week leading up to your group interaction on this chapter. Come to the meeting prepared to share with the group at least one way that your prayer was answered.

2. If you are comfortable doing so, bring something to the meeting that reminds you of the greatness of God. Maybe it is a song by a Christian artist. Perhaps it is a favorite praise song that the group can sing together. It could be a poem or a favorite Scripture. Maybe it is a photo from a family vacation or a special item from your childhood. Share the significance of this item as it relates to your spiritual life.

3. Do you think contemporary Christians tend to over emphasize or undervalue angels? Why? How should Christians respond to the current emphasis on angels in print media, television and film? See the College Press website, www.collegepress.com, for resources that will help provide a balanced biblical view of angels.

4. What is one life-issue that you find challenging to keep in proper perspective? Share that issue with the group. As a group, pray for one another regarding these items. Adopt one person to pray for (about this specific issue) between now and the next meeting.

Memory Verse
Hebrews 1:8

But about the Son he says, "Your throne, O God, will last for ever and ever, and righteousness will be the scepter of your kingdom."

A LEADER FOR THE JOURNEY

HEBREWS 2:5–3:6

You can't celebrate Christmas without thinking about journeys. Often the travel talk is captured in a song. Over the radio or department store speakers come the words of "There's No Place Like Home for the Holidays." Soon, you find yourself inevitably thinking about home and how or when you are going to get there. Perhaps you cannot travel during the season. Your longing is captured in "I'll Be Home for the Christmas," and you vow to travel mentally if not physically. Whether you shop for Christmas in town or across the state, you are confronted with people on pilgrimage. You hum "Silver Bells" to yourself and traffic jams are experienced with holiday cheer. Rudolph wasn't commissioned so Santa could just sit there. Even Frosty the Snowman takes kids on a hike through town. The wonder of the season is captured through travel tunes.

> There are plenty of journeys in
> the original Christmas story, too.

There are plenty of journeys in the original Christmas story, too. We don't sing about them as much, which is too bad. Eternally significant stuff happened when these trips were taken. Mary headed to Judean hill country so two pregnant relatives could rejoice together in the Lord's blessing upon them and the world (Luke 1:39-56). Joseph and Mary traveled to Bethlehem so that Micah 5:2 might be fulfilled (Luke 2:4). The magi represented in "We Three Kings" didn't exactly live next to the inn. They "traversed afar" (Matt 2:1-2). (No, they didn't get there in time to make the real nativity scene. Have you ever noticed how many Christmas songs they end up in, though?) The shepherds got there quickly, though, and they received the word while in fields outside Bethlehem (Luke 2:8, 15-16). Jesus was just getting used to his surroundings when Mary and Joseph took him to Jerusalem for the first time (Luke 2:22). While we don't usually sing the travel talk directly, it is implied in virtually every Christian carol. So much for singing about Frosty's corncob pipe. Some journeys change the world.

> ### Some journeys change the world.

Jesus' journey transcended all others in both scope and significance, so we celebrate by marveling aloud. Yet, here's the odd thing. We struggle to accept the implications of sermons we sing to ourselves. Max Lucado captures the paradox of it all.

> He came, not as a flash of light or as an unapproachable conqueror, but as one whose first cries were heard by a peasant girl and a sleepy carpenter. The hands that first held him were unmanicured, callused, and dirty. No silk. No ivory. No hype. No party. No hoopla. . . . Angels watched as Mary changed God's diaper. The universe watched with wonder as the Almighty learned to walk. Children played in the street with him. And had the synagogue leader in Nazareth known who was listening to his sermons. . . . For thirty-three years he would feel everything you and I have ever felt. He felt weak. He grew weary. He was afraid of failure. He was susceptible to wooing women. He got colds, burped and had body odor. His feelings got hurt. His feet got tired. And his head ached. To think of Jesus in such a light is—well, it seems almost irreverent, doesn't it? It's not something we like to do; it's uncomfortable. It is much easier to keep the humanity out of the incarnation. . . . He's easier to stomach that way. There is something about keeping him divine that keeps him distant, packaged, predictable. But don't do it. For heaven's sake, don't. Let him be as human as he intended to be. Let him into the muck and mire of our world. *For only if we let him in can he pull us out* (Italics mine).[1]

Psalm 8 communicates essentially the same message in similarly striking fashion. Hebrews 2 contains a Christmas carol, you see. In its original context, the Psalm addresses humanity's lofty status as the crown jewel of God's creation. Out of all God's earthly creatures, people were given the responsibility of protecting God's creation and the dignity of reflecting God's image (Gen 1:26-28). The Psalmist doesn't

27

‡

C
H
A
P
T
E
R

just want us to grasp the truth, he wants us to feel his tone. This is a song of celebration, full of mystery and wonder. And, if events stayed where the Psalm stops, it could remain that way.

When mankind sinned and fell short of God's intent, however, things changed. Both interpersonal relationships and the harmony between humanity and nature were fractured (Gen 3:16-19). All creation needed a new leader—someone who would restore God's original design for people and restore the full wonder of Psalm 8. Hebrews 2:10-18 shows Jesus is that leader. He could not fulfill God's plans for people without fully becoming a person; therefore, he strategically and temporarily became lower than the angels he had spoken into existence (v. 9). These verses explain why.

The message is presented through four distinct but interrelated images. Each builds upon the themes established prior to it and anticipates those that follow.

Jesus Is Our Trailblazing Leader (2:10)

In order for us to understand this verse, two terms need clarification. First, the word *author* actually has a wide range of possible meanings. This verse is probably showing that Jesus is both our pioneer (one who goes where others have not) and our trailblazer (one who clears a path where there was none). The accent, I think, is on the latter. Second, Hebrews uses *perfect* in a special sense. It means that a person is fully qualified for a particular task. This verse does not primarily emphasize Jesus' sinlessness (though this truth is very important in the overall message of the book). Rather, it shows that Jesus' complete experience of humanity, including death, was a necessity for his trailblazing task.

Jesus is both our pioneer and our trailblazer.

Jesus' majesty (chapter 1) and manhood (chapter 2) are complementary rather than contradictory characteristics. As the portrait of God's essence and the expression of his power, Jesus was well acquainted with the glorious presence of God. It was his permanent address for eternity past. Without becoming human, however, Jesus would have been trying to blaze a trail from a place he never went to a place he never left. That's a little like trying to blaze a trail from the heart of Kansas into Missouri without ever leaving St. Louis (okay, I said a *little*). He descended to us so that we could ascend with him. Far from being a logical inconsistency, the incarnation was a logical necessity.

These truths are indeed a wonder. What we needed was someone who could enter the overgrown terrain of our world so that a clear path could be created from us to God. God himself made it happen.

These truths are also a warning. The terms were determined according to what was fitting according to the mind of God (2:10), not the minds of people. The point is not that Jesus is *an* appropriate trailblazer, but that he is *the* appropriate trailblazer. Those who choose another pioneer are on the wrong path.

Jesus Is Our Identifying Leader (2:11-13)

By employing family imagery, Hebrews makes the strongest possible statement about the depth of Jesus' love for and loyalty to God's people. Family relationships were even more central and defining in the first-century world than they are in the contemporary western world. Bringing shame on one's family was the greatest social blunder one could commit. Hearing that Jesus was not ashamed to identify with them as family would have impacted these Christians more than we can fathom. It is also a great encouragement for us, however, because it shows Jesus isn't bashful about his brothers and sisters.

The text establishes this concept through two Old Testament passages that share three common denominators. Each of the similarities reinforces ideas established in verse 10, while communicating them through family imagery.

> Hebrews makes the strongest possible statement about the depth of Jesus' love for and loyalty to God's people.

First, the reality of suffering flavors both passages. Early Christians recognized numerous connections between Psalm 22 and Jesus' crucifixion (the Psalm begins, for example, with "My God, My God, why have you forsaken me?"). Isaiah 8:17-18, on the other hand, was written at a time when Israel was facing oppression from a foreign superpower. Second, each text describes the speaker as faithful and/or trusting. The writer puts these words in Jesus' mouth, because his actions articulated them. Third, both contain specific statements that specifically locate the speaker in the presence of family members.

Jesus did not take a mercenary mentality toward his trailblazing task. He was not like a tour guide, trail guide, or cab driver who creates an illusion of identification while remaining safely detached on the journey. We can rejoice that God's appointed means of blazing a trail was achieved in a personal way. We can also rejoice that it was achieved with a personal touch.

Jesus Is Our Liberating Leader (2:14-16)

These verses are reminders that Jesus' identification with us was strategic, not sentimental. His liberation frees us from the devil (v. 14) and death (v. 15).

The term translated *destroy* does not mean that the devil no longer exists; rather, his work has been nullified by Jesus' work. The devil desires to lead people into sin and the consequence of sin is death (Rom 6:23). Through his death, Jesus trumped the devil's best card and overcame his most imposing weapon. When we think of Jesus bringing about Satan's demise, the resurrection typically comes to mind. Even Paul's eloquent presentation of our resurrection hope contains 24 references to death (1 Corinthian 15). It is hard to have the former without the latter!

Statistics indicate that about one fifth of the American population list death as their greatest fear. The top answer overall is fear of public speaking, which is listed number one by about one fourth of those surveyed. As Jerry Seinfeld observed, apparently Americans think it is better to be in the casket than delivering the eulogy! Based on my ministry experiences, I'm a little suspicious of such surveys. I haven't had to spend much time praying with folks who are unnerved by an upcoming presentation, and I teach both preaching and speech. With folks who are facing the reality of their mortality, it is a different story. I would guess most of those who highlighted public speaking probably came out of their last heath checkup feeling pretty good.

30

‡

C
H
A
P
T
E
R

There are numerous reasons why people fear death, and an authentic relationship with God through Christ can address all of them. In this passage, however, there are two primary ways that Jesus' liberating work alleviates common causes for such fear. First, by dying to pay the price for our sin, Jesus has taken away the Christian's fear of death's eternal consequences. Hebrews 9–10 especially emphasizes this. Second, because Jesus has blazed the trail, we do not have to fear the unknown. While we have not experienced death directly, he has and can help us through that stage of our journey.

You don't have to be a political science or history major to know that liberated people celebrate. Have you ever wondered what it would be like to have experienced the streets of Paris or Baghdad at such moments? For Christians, celebrating our freedom should be a daily event in which the greatest liberation receives the greatest response.

Jesus Is Our Empathizing Leader (2:17-18)

These verses function as a transition in Hebrews and anticipate key ideas that will be developed more completely in the central section of the book (4:14–10:18). There are eight words or phrases that are paralleled just in 4:14–5:3, for example. These ideas are addressed later in our study, so let's just pause at this stage and focus on a single factor that is especially addressed here and in 4:14-16. It wasn't enough for Jesus to associate with us. He had to understand us. On his earthly journey, Jesus learned to see and experience life from the vantage point of humans.

Perhaps in a moment of especially strong temptation or unusually severe frustration on your journey you have prayed, "God, you just don't know what it is like to be me." At first, this seems like a reasonable statement. After all, like the priest in the movie *Rudy* says, "God is God, and we are not." Jesus did not learn what it was like to commit sin, but he learned more about the power of temptation than any of us ever will. The reason, as observed by C.S. Lewis in *Mere Christianity*, is simple: we give in to temptation before it reaches maximum strength. No, we don't give in to temptation every time. All of us, however, give in to sin at some point (Rom 3:23). No one but Jesus knows how strong temptation can become, because he is the only one who has experienced its full potential.

Of course, Jesus has not experienced the specific temptation to repeat a sin, but that isn't the point. He is our best possible help in times of trouble, because he personally understands the dynamics of temptation and has emerged victorious over it. As William Willimon observes, when we face temptation, Jesus is able to say "that reminds me of the time. . . ."[2]

> He is our best possible help in times of trouble, because he personally understands the dynamics of temptation and has emerged victorious over it.

This is perhaps one of the most difficult elements of Jesus' journey to absorb. We (or at least I) default toward envisioning Jesus as if he encountered people with a holy mental detachment. There is a clear difference, of course, between saying that Jesus was tempted to sin and saying Jesus sinned. Yet, in my mental pictures of Jesus, I sometimes struggle to acknowledge the distinction. I want to see a Jesus so separated from sin that he didn't even know what the sinful options were. I'm not suggesting Jesus failed to be above sin in his thought life. That contradicts the message of Scripture in general and Hebrews in particular. I am reminding myself that Jesus' journey wasn't as easy as I sometimes fantasize. The more I think about it, I'm glad. Aren't you?

> **Christmas was the beginning of Jesus' journey, but it should be celebrated every day of ours.**

If we can really grasp the significance of these verses, it will change what we sing this Christmas. It will change how we sing this Christmas. It may even change to whom we sing this Christmas. In fact, it will change the way we sing all year. Christmas was the beginning of Jesus' journey, but it should be celebrated every day of ours. 🔲

---

[1] Max Lucado, *God Came Near* (Portland: Multnomah Press, 1989), 27.
[2] William Willimon, "You Need a Good Priest." Audiocassette. Preaching Today.

Activities for Your Group's Journey

1. Which of the four portraits of Jesus in Hebrews 2:10-18 (trailblazing, identifying, liberating, or empathizing leader) is the most meaningful to you today? Why? Is there another of these images that has been more meaningful at a different stage of your life? If so, why?

2. Are any of these pictures (or the implications of these pictures) difficult for you to understand or acknowledge? For example, is it difficult to acknowledge that Jesus fully experienced death? That he is the only liberator from the devil/death? That he is truly unashamed to be family with us? That he authentically experienced temptation? If so, why?

3. Do you think God wants Christians to think about their own mortality? What are the benefits of thinking about death? What are the possible dangers of doing so?

4. What are some creative ways you can employ the concepts from Hebrews 2 into your Christmas celebration this year? If your group is studying this material near the holiday season, perhaps you could plan a Christmas party incorporating some of these pictures.

5. Think about a specific non-Christian you know. Which of these four pictures of Jesus would especially help you communicate the gospel to that particular person? Pray for one another as a group, asking God to provide an opportunity for each group member to do so. When he does, take advantage of it.

Memory Verse
Hebrews 2:17-18

For this reason he had to be made like his brothers in every way, in order that he might become a merciful and faithful high priest in service to God, and that he might make atonement for the sins of the people. [18]Because he himself suffered when he was tempted, he is able to help those who are being tempted.

33

‡

C
H
A
P
T
E
R

A Leader for the Journey 3

CHAPTER FOUR

PEACE FOR THE JOURNEY

HEBREWS 3:1–4:13

Have you ever been on a trip where you desperately longed for real rest? When on family excursions, we try to keep the kids' spirits up by reminding them of how nice it will be to stay in a hotel. Our efforts are only moderately successful. You see, I am a sucker for hotels that have words like "budget" worked right into the title. When we travel, the *modus operandi* is to find a safe, clean, inexpensive hotel. This tendency tempers the kids' expectations regarding our resting place, and it often produces a less than peaceful journey. Instead, it spawns nightmares of rooms without hot water pressure, towels and carpet made from 40-grain sandpaper, lumpy mattresses, washcloth-sized pillows, televisions with rabbit ear antennas . . . you get the picture. When your final destination isn't especially appealing, it messes up the whole trip. On the other hand, knowing there is rest at the end of the journey can bring peace in the midst of the journey.

Last year we attended a military graduation in Pensacola. Knowing a fourteen-hour trip awaited, we began preemptive psychological warfare almost immediately. We painted mental murals describing the marvels of our hotel, but the kids were understandably suspicious. They know their father well. This time, however, my sister-in-law had obtained our rooms. This, plus knowing the words "Grand Hotel" were contained in the title, gave the kids hope.

Remember the moment when Willy Wonka's guests first enter his chocolate factory? That's what we looked like as we entered through the revolving glass doors. Polished marble floors led to polished fruit in polished glass bowls beside polished brass elevator doors. We didn't stay in the Presidential Suite, but we aren't used to hotels that even have a Presidential Suite. We didn't eat at either of the two restaurants, but we are used to staying in places where the only food is in vending machines with a retro pull-knob. We didn't use the exercise room, but we are used to places where you get exercise from carrying the bags up two flights of stairs, past the laundry machines, and through a labyrinth of hallways.

We directly experienced other perks, however. Working the shower nozzle required a degree in mechanical engineering to maximize its potential. The television set had a kazillion working channels, the carpeting and towels were plush, and beds were delightful. The sky-lit, fountain-filled atrium was nice, as was the Grand Ballroom across the corridor. The highlight, though, was enjoying cheesecake and coffee in the library. Yes, the hotel had a library. Yes, people are allowed to eat and drink there. Waiters in black bow ties brought the dessert to us. Honestly, I could hardly keep from doing a happy dance. Julie Andrews can have "raindrops on roses and whiskers on kittens." Cheesecake, coffee, books (and even bow ties) are a few of my favorite things.

Our stay was most restful. It also transformed the way our kids think about places of rest. On subsequent trips, I've noticed they are much more interested in where we will be stopping for the night. When they anticipate the destination, the whole trip goes better. Knowing you'll rest well at the end of the journey gives peace in the midst of the journey.

> **Knowing you'll rest well at the end of the journey gives peace in the midst of the journey.**

A promise of rest comprises the heart of Hebrews 3–4. In these chapters, the writer of Hebrews weaves together Old Testament quotes, allusions to Old Testament events, and appeals to Old Testament examples. The result is a portrait of Jesus as provider of ultimate rest. Such rest is precisely what Jesus promised his followers in Matthew 11:27-28 when he said, "Come to me, you who are weary and heavy laden, and I will give you rest." The sound of an ultimate rest stop on our journey through life does sound rather appealing, doesn't it?

Maybe you are longing for *physical rest*. If so, you are not alone. According to the National Sleep Foundation, we are a sleep-deprived nation.

33% of adults sleep less than 6½ hours nightly.
51% indicate sleepiness on the job interferes with the amount of work they get done.

19% report making occasional or frequent work errors due to sleepiness.

24% report difficulty getting up for work more than one day per week.

43% say sleepiness interferes with their daily activities at least three days per week.[1]

Since there are lots of tired people out there, maybe we all just need a nap. After all, one of Webster's definitions for sleep is "rest."

There's just one problem. Some folks get plenty of sleep, but they are not at rest. One leading indicator of depression, for example, is a dramatically increased amount of sleep. I've also met people in nursing homes who are well acquainted with their pillows but consider serenity a stranger. Please understand—I'm in favor of naps. I certainly don't want to get on the wrong side of the National Sleep Foundation! There has to be more to rest than sleep, however.

There has to be more to rest than sleep.

Maybe you are longing for emotional or psychological rest. A break from the routine or freedom from a stressful environment is what you desire. Stress is certainly taking its toll on the American workforce. An estimated 300 billion dollars is lost annually due to stress-related issues such as compensation claims, reduced productivity, absenteeism, medical expenses, and employee turnover.[2]

The impact is also felt at home. Scott Grant tells of a mother who sent the following note to the attendance secretary of Southside High School in Rockville Centre, NY.

> Please excuse the absence of my daughter. She has been suffering from a severe head cold. Since she has been home, she has consumed 18 doughnuts, three quart containers of orange juice, a half-gallon of cranberry juice, four two-liter bottles of Diet Coke, about 30 Pop-tarts, and all the family's Christmas candy canes. MTV has been blasting incessantly. The house is knee-deep in used Kleenex. Today, Fed Ex delivered seven Chia pets and four boxes containing the clapper she ordered from the Home Shopping Channel. With the thermostat set at 78 degrees, I need extra fuel delivery, and the wallpaper has peeled off the bathroom as a result of her hourly therapeutic sauna baths. Our cat is in a state of shock from being repeatedly bombarded with Hall's mentholated cough drops. Although she is not exactly 100 percent yet, she will attend school today. Please do not send her home unless she lapses into a coma. I need a break.[3]

Perhaps we all just need a vacation. After all, one of Webster's definitions for vacation is "taking a break from work or studies for rest."

Here's the problem, though. Have you ever embarked on a getaway, only to discover upon your return that you need a vacation from your vacation? Furthermore, while stress is a substantial concern, alleviation of stress doesn't automatically bring peace. Some folks are as restless in their retirement as they were during their working years. There must be more to rest than simply a vacation.

While we might desire physical and psychological rest, what we most require is *spiritual rest*. In the 400s A.D. a Christian named Augustine observed, "Our souls remain restless until they find their rest in Thee." He was saying we have a God-shaped void that is a God-given void. Therefore, it only makes sense that our longing for rest is also a God-filled void.

> "Our souls remain restless until they find their rest in Thee."

God created us with the capacity for a harmonious relationship with himself. Until we experience reconciliation with him, there is a sense of spiritual restlessness deep within. Some people deny this inner striving, while others attempt to alleviate the angst through relationships, hobbies, or religious rituals. As these verses demonstrate, however, receiving true rest requires embracing Jesus. He is like a new Moses (3:1-6) who delivers people from spiritual bondage. He is like a new Joshua (4:7-11) who leads people to a place of spiritual blessing.

Hebrews 3–4 challenges us to enter and enjoy spiritual rest. By considering three major emphases in these chapters, we can position ourselves to experience peace on the journey.

The Nature of God's Rest

Spiritual rest is a challenging concept to grasp; therefore, the writer of Hebrews uses two analogies that were familiar to his audience. Rest, he says, is like an ongoing Sabbath or Israel's possession of Canaan. The rest Jesus provides is greater, however. In fact, the core issues that made Sabbath and Canaan such significant blessings for Jews receive their fullest expression in the gifts Jesus makes available to us.

For example, both Sabbath and Canaan were by-products of Israel's status as God's people. Sabbath wasn't simply a day off, and Canaan wasn't simply a homeland. They were gifts from God, provided as a by-product of Israel's covenant relationship with him. Therefore, "rest" in Hebrews 3–4 is specifically a spiritual blessing. It is much more than a Sunday afternoon spent in a hammock. Anyone can experience that kind of rest. Both Sabbath and Canaan were divinely designed to distinguish Israel from nations that didn't worship God. Our experience of rest similarly sets us apart from non-Christians.

Furthermore, both Sabbath and Canaan involved the ceasing of particular kinds of effort. Jewish Sabbath practices required stepping away from the daily routine, just as God's rest in Genesis 2:2 signified the conclusion to his creating activity. Israel's entrance to Canaan provided a cessation to the work of partnering with God to take the land. Similarly, Jesus' offer of rest includes the ceasing of certain kinds of work. Specifically, as the context of Jesus' statement in Matthew 11:27–28 indicates, we are freed from the burden of striving to manufacture a right relationship with God.

Finally, both Sabbath and Canaan were holistic blessings that were by-products of a meaningful relationship with God. They provided an overall sense of contentment, security, and peace. The rest Jesus provides is similarly a comprehensive result of our salvation. Knowing we are in a harmonious relationship with God impacts every area of our lives. Our spiritual, emotional and physical components are inseparably intertwined. Therefore, the concepts of physical and emotional rest are not as far removed from Hebrews 3–4 as it might seem. For example, a right relationship with God and an ongoing commitment to trusting God remove much anxiety. This, in turn, helps us sleep better. It is crucial to remember, however, that the wellspring of such blessings is the forgiveness Jesus provides.

The Availability of Rest

The theoretical idea of rest doesn't mean much if it is not accessible to us. The numerous references to Psalm 95 in Hebrews 3–4 demonstrate that the opportunity for rest is not relegated to ancient history. Joshua led Israel into Canaan about 600 years before David wrote this Psalm, yet David said a rest was available later—it is available *today*. The offer of this rest *today* shows it is available to us. In other words, the writer of Hebrews says our era of life is included within the category of what David meant by "today." We can enter God's rest in the present. We can begin experiencing the by-products of salvation, a spiritual land of Canaan, in the here and now. Knowing we will rest well at the end of the journey can bring us peace in the midst of the journey.

At the same time, our rest culminates in the future (Rev 14:13). We anticipate a day in which our redemption is fully and finally realized. Similarly, the fullest experience of our spiritual rest comes in the New Jerusalem. Even the most obedient, committed Christian faces spiritual struggles in the present. There will come a day, however, when our striving will cease. Then, we will experience ongoing, ultimate blessing as a result of our relationship with God through Christ.

Entering God's Rest

How, then, can we enter such a blessed state of rest? Hebrews 4:11-13 provides the answer and the example of Israel provides an illustration. The answer is paradoxical. We enter God's rest by exerting ourselves. The kind of effort the writer has in view, however, is not an effort to impress God with our efforts. Rather, our exertion is evidence of authentic, active faith. Such obedient trust in God is a prerequisite to peace, because it is the means by which we embrace his offer of spiritual rest.

The example of Israel helps clarify the paradox. God told the Israelites he was giving them Canaan, and spies were sent to evaluate the land (Numbers 13). Upon their return the spies presented a report consisting of two main points. The first point was that the land was indeed bountiful. The second point was that the current inhabitants were large and their cities well fortified. At that point the Israelites had a choice to make. With the exception of Caleb and Joshua, the nation chose to disobey God and trust their own wisdom regarding the best course of action. By refusing to obey God, they forfeited the good news of an awaiting rest (Heb 4:2). From that point forward, this generation of Israelites was used as an example of the peril that befalls those failing to trust God (Heb 3:7-11).

By considering their example, we are challenged to respond positively to God's message. For those who do so, his message contains the promise of rest. For those who trust their own counsel over God's commands, God's penetrating word becomes a word of judgment (Heb 4:12-13). As a result, the opportunity for spiritual rest is forfeited.

How will you respond to God's offer of rest?

How will you respond to God's offer of rest? Believe it or not, he is more interested in your restfulness than you are! He wants to provide you with a peaceful journey on the way to his ultimate rest. Knowing your destination is both secure and sensational can provide a peace that transcends the perils of your pathway. Trust him by obeying the gospel. Trust him by following his guidance each day thereafter. On our journey, the only way to travel at peace is to travel with the Prince of Peace.

---

[1] "National Sleep Foundation Releases New Statistics on Sleep in America." Internet.
[2] "Corporate Stress Solutions: Stress Statistics." Internet.
[3] Scott Grant, "Resting with God," sermoncentral.com.

Activities for Your Group's Journey

1. Spend some time reflecting on the idea of salvation as spiritual rest. How can this rest imagery help us communicate the gospel in our culture?

2. Though all Christians are spiritually at rest, there are differences in the degrees to which believers experience the inner peace that is a by-product of salvation. What factors contribute to this difference? What practical steps can we take to insure the most peaceful of journeys?

3. What do you most eagerly anticipate about heaven and the culmination of your spiritual rest?

4. Spend some time as a group praying for those members who are especially in need of spiritual rest.

For the word of God is living and active. Sharper than any double-edged sword, it penetrates even to dividing soul and spirit, joints and marrow; it judges the thoughts and attitudes of the heart.

CHAPTER FIVE

WARNINGS FOR THE JOURNEY

HEBREWS 5:11–6:20

Spiritual lessons can surface from the most surprising sources. Yesterday, I made a trip to Wal-Mart. For some folks, trips to Wal-Mart are a daily devotional experience. Sam Walton, John Boy Walton—they are all the same to me. Nevertheless, our fifteen water jugs needed to be refilled, so off I went. Visions of distant parking locations, long checkout lines, and overly talkative greeters filled my mind.

I found a parking spot within reasonable walking distance and headed toward the water machine. A quick glance at the checkout lines suggested this might be an unusually good trip. With growing optimism, I glanced toward the greeter's station. I suppose two out of three isn't bad. This greeter was overqualified for the job. He wasn't just a greeter, he was a certified conversationalist. Plus, he was in catharsis mode. The subject? His most recent trip to the doctor. I tried to appear busy. When filling water jugs, however, it is fairly hard to get that otherworldly, focused look.

He started with an inventory of clothing articles he had been asked to remove. Apparently something in my expression inadvertently indicated interest. Therefore, he continued with an itemized list of body parts that had received pushing and probing. Apparently my body language unintentionally cried out, "Please give me more. I know you are withholding information from me, Captain Catharsis. I've got to have all the details." So, he rehashed the recommendations provided by his doctor.

He wants me to change my diet. Are you kidding? My taste buds are the only part of my body that still works. No way I'm changing my diet. He wants me to exercise. Are you kidding? I walk from the recliner to the refrigerator three or four times a night. He wants me to take vitamins. Are you kidding? Why would I take vitamins? If I had money to spend on things like that, I wouldn't be working at Wal-Mart. No sir, I've been around the block a time or two and it seems like the trip is going just fine.

On the drive home, I kept hearing echoes of the greeter's voice. He seems like a pretty nice guy, but I've got a feeling his journey is headed down a treacherous trail. From his perspective the trip is going just fine, so he doesn't want to hear a well-informed and well-timed word of warning. Guess what? I'm more like him than I would like to admit. Perhaps you are as well.

This section of Hebrews is good advice from the Great Physician. It warns us of what can happen when we place our lives in positions of spiritual risk. Strategically set between two discussions regarding the nature of Jesus' high priestly ministry, this extended exhortation challenges believers to hold firmly to the salvation made available through Christ.

I'll admit it up front. This is not the most enjoyable section of our study. Warnings are intended to be productive, not pleasant. Let's view this material from the right perspective, though. In the midst of grave warnings is God's goodness. Good doctors tell patients what they need to hear, regardless of what they want to hear. Such is the truest expression of concern God could provide.

> Warnings are intended to be productive, not pleasant.
> In the midst of grave warnings is God's goodness.

The writer of Hebrews mirrors God's mind-set in these verses, which have two primary emphases. First, the symptoms that evidence dangerous spiritual conditions are highlighted. Then the end results of one's spiritual condition are considered. Each is provided as a catalyst to spiritual growth.

Marks of Immaturity (5:11-14)

Some of these believers' lives evidenced a lack of spiritual progress reflected in three interrelated symptoms. By considering these criteria, we can take stock of our own spiritual condition.

The first symptom of spiritual struggle is a *lack of interest*. This absence of passion for God is described in the phrase *slow to learn*

(5:11). The statement is a little confusing. When we describe a learner as slow, it is typically an evaluation of the person's intellectual capacity. Here, however, the issue is commitment rather than capability. The phrase literally carries the idea of a person having lazy ears. The problem was not that they couldn't hear, but that they wouldn't hear. They were challenged in Hebrews 2:1 to pay more careful attention to what they had already heard. They didn't need new information; they needed a fresh commitment to what they had already received.

Our interest level, you see, impacts our hearing. It is true in all areas of life. Students who are interested in the subject matter typically pay the closest attention in class. Children usually listen more closely to instructions regarding the family vacation than those involving the family cleaning day. The radio can blare all day without anyone really listening, but a news bulletin, weather warning, or special song can suddenly improve the auditory capabilities of an entire office. Our hearing reflects our heart.

> Our interest level, you see, impacts our hearing.
> Our hearing reflects our heart.

So, here's the question. How interested are you in hearing from God? Are you interested enough to buy Bible study software? Sure it is expensive. So are computer games. Are you interested enough to attend a conference? Sure it takes time. So do golfing and shopping expeditions. Are you interested enough to be consistent in home group involvement? Sure it might shorten the Sunday afternoon nap. So does television programming. Here's the bottom line. Our willingness to listen to God is a barometer of our commitment to God. So what do your ears say about you?

> What do your ears say about you?

A lack of spiritual interest leads directly to a lack of *spiritual growth*. These verses provide spiritual shock treatment to these believers by demonstrating the absurdity of their present status. There's no mistaking it. The two statements made here regarding their spiritual health are insulting and degrading. The goal is lofty, however. God is working through this material to help people see the seriousness of their status. He uses imagery from first-century philosophical schools to make his point.

The first image comes from the term translated *elementary teachings*. It was used to describe the ABCs of a given philosophy, and the point is that these people need to learn them once again. What an insult! Picture a group of Ivy League English majors singing the alphabet song in an effort to keep the letters straight. A mechanic running to his/her manuals to see where the oil goes. A scoutmaster struggling with the intricacies of the square knot. A chef trying to remember the difference between broiling and baking. A computer science major struggling to set up an e-mail account. That's the picture of these folks in their spiritual development.

The next imagery involves comparison between *milk* and *solid food*. This language was used in philosophical schools to describe the difference between topics a new convert could handle compared to those a more advanced student was ready for. Imagine going to a black tie/black dress banquet and having to take your baby formula along—not for your child but for yourself! Can you fathom bypassing filet mignon in favor of menu-by-Gerber? That is the spiritual condition in which some of these folks found themselves. They had an opportunity to feast on the finest spiritual food, but their ongoing infancy prohibited doing so.

> Can you fathom bypassing filet mignon
> in favor of menu-by-Gerber?

Hebrews 6:1-3 lists the details of their diet. The six items mentioned are considered basics because each contains a significant underlying connection between Christianity and Judaism. These elements of Jewish teaching (viewed in light of Christ's coming) show how one is saved from the past, serves in the present, and is evaluated in the future. The writer of Hebrews wasn't asking these folks to set aside these common denominators between Christianity and Judaism. Meals of milk and the alphabet song are good places to start. They are also poor places to stop, and that is apparently what some of these folks were doing.

So, how is your spiritual digestive system? Lots of folks are in desperate need of a spiritual growth spurt. Our Christian conversations often boil down to questions like, "How long have you been a Christian?" or "How long have you been attending this church?" The writer of Hebrews is challenging us to demonstrate mature lives in Christ, not simply miles logged with Christ. It is heartbreaking to see folks who have been Christians for decades but only know the Bible verses they learned in elementary school. Even in small group interaction, our participation can become painfully predictable. God desires more for us and from us.

Such spiritual stagnation results in a lack of *spiritual discernment*. Biblical truth is not merely provided to help us win trivia games and solve crossword puzzles. God's truth helps us make the right decisions in everyday life. Paul indicated Scripture was useful for teaching correct doctrine, correcting wrong doctrine, teaching correct behavior, and correcting wrong behavior (2 Tim 3:16-17). Hebrews 5:13 reinforces this idea, reminding us that Scripture helps us negotiate the doctrinal and ethical crossroads of life. Without advancing in our faith, however, we lack the framework from which to make such decisions.

Do you live more wisely this year than you did last year? Are ethical decisions made from a more informed perspective than they were when you first became a Christian? Are you better able to wrestle through such issues on your own, or do you still need a guide at every crossroad on the journey? Such questions help us determine whether we are growing up or are simply growing older.

> Such questions help us determine whether
> we are growing up or are simply growing older.

Motivations for Maturity (6:4-20)

Having helped his hearers see the reality of their current condition, the writer motivates them (and us) toward a better future. He does so by demonstrating the natural by-products of our spiritual choices.

A Word of Warning (Heb 6:4-8)

The worst-case scenario is presented first. The writer's highest concern involves the possibility of people falling away, thereby making themselves unable to express repentance.

It is sometimes suggested that this warning is irrelevant to the authentically converted. Accordingly, the warning must be directed toward those who haven't actually made a true commitment to Christ. It appears that the warning has significance for Christians, however, for two reasons. First, those who "fall away" are unable to be renewed to repentance (NIV, *brought back to repentance*). This implies they have repented on a previous occasion. Second, the five phrases in Hebrews 6:4-5 indicate Christians are in view, although it might not seem so at first reading. The term *enlightened* is found in 10:32 and was used in the early church to describe the completion of the conversion process at baptism. The term *tasted* was used at 2:9 to describe Jesus' full experience of death; therefore, it doesn't mean a person who simply nibbles around the edges of Christianity. The term *shared* is used in Hebrews 3:1, 14 to describe those who possess the benefits and by-products of salvation. Therefore, it appears those in danger of falling away are part of the faith community. Because the passage is a source of much debate and a seedbed for much confusion, a few other observations are in order.

First, this passage is talking about a person reaching a condition where they have no desire to turn back to God. It is not a matter of God's willingness to forgive, it is a matter of the person's willingness to repent.

> It is not a matter of God's willingness to forgive,
> it is a matter of the person's willingness to repent.

Second, we are talking about something drastic here. The term "fall away" is used in church lingo to describe people in all kinds of conditions. This verse, however, addresses someone who no longer acknowledges and responds to the unique claims of Jesus. Therefore, "falling away" doesn't happen nearly so easily and often as we are sometimes inclined to think. The persons in view are facing the temptation to revert from Christianity back to Judaism. This text (and many others throughout Hebrews) demonstrate that doing so is equivalent to idolatry (since it involves rejecting Jesus).

Finally, the passage is probably dealing with the *current* condition of the "fallen" more than the broader concern of whether or not such a person can repent. The NIV translates the two phrases in Hebrews 6:6 with an emphasis on the term *because*. This is an interpretation on the translators' part that is not required by the grammar of the passage. It should perhaps be translated *since* rather than *because*. Understood in this fashion, the text is saying one cannot authentically repent before God so long as the significance of Jesus' work is being denied. It is not enough to be truly sorry for one's sin. The only means by which one can authentically repent requires embracing Jesus. The Jews who originally crucified and humiliated Jesus were followers of God. They just didn't accept Jesus as Messiah. For these Jewish Christians, the challenge is to avoid making the same mistake as their forefathers did when Jesus walked the earth.

Here's the bottom line. Failure to grow in our faith makes us vulnerable in even the fundamentals of our faith. By not moving beyond the basics, we can hamstring our growth to such a degree that we may reach a point where we no longer believe the basics. Hearing such a warning can be disconcerting. Sometimes, however, such shock treatment is exactly what is needed.

> By not moving beyond the basics,
> we can hamstring our growth.

A Word of Encouragement (6:9-20)

The writer of Hebrews also motivates through encouragement. His reassuring words are based on the character of God and the conduct of these believers. Both elements can provide encouragement for us as well.

First, the example of these Hebrew Christians is noted. By their fruitfulness, they have demonstrated the life transformation that evidences salvation (Heb 6:7-9). This is a way for the writer of Hebrews to affirm that they are currently among the saved. While the warning is real, so is the authenticity of their faith. Even if no one else sees their efforts, God does. Even though no one else can perfectly assess their spiritual condition, God can. He verifies they are on the right path and challenges them to continue on that path. May the same be said of us.

Second, the character of God is stressed. The previous verses have demonstrated the writer's confidence in his audience; now, he expresses ultimate confidence in God. Like an anchor, God's trustworthiness is a source of stability and security in our lives. The only ineffective anchor is the one that is pulled out or never put in. These verses, therefore, challenge believers to partner with God so they can have assurance regarding their hope in Christ (5:12).

> The only ineffective anchor is the one
> that is pulled out or never put in.

As I read this passage of Scripture, my mind keeps going back to the greeter by the water machine. The lesson God taught me through that encounter is really pretty simple. Ignored warnings are ineffective warnings. Since the goal of spiritual diagnosis is spiritual health, both accurate assessment and a resolute response are required. Only the Holy Spirit is fully capable of providing an accurate diagnosis. Our response to his affirmation and admonition will determine God's assessment of our journey. When he evaluates our lives, I pray he can say, in the words of my Wal-Mart friend, "The trip is going just fine." ⊞

Activities for Your Group's Journey

1. Do you know anyone who once claimed to be a Christian and now practices another religion? What brought about the change and why? Were the symptoms of spiritual struggle (5:11–6:3) evident in their lives?

2. Most Christians appear to experience times when their spiritual interest-level drops. Is that your experience? What can we do to prepare ourselves in advance? How can we maintain stability during such seasons of our lives? Are there preventive measures we can take to avoid such lulls? If so, what are they?

3. If you have experienced a significant spiritual lull at some point, reflect back on that experience. How did God work in your life to bring you out of that down period?

4. How do you respond to warning passages such as the one in Hebrews 6:4-6? Do you find such warnings discouraging and deflating? Or do they strengthen your resolve and commitment? How should we respond to those who are tempted to give up when they hear such passages?

Memory Verse
Hebrews 6:11-12

We want each of you to show this same diligence to the very end, in order to make your hope sure. ¹²We do not want you to become lazy, but to imitate those who through faith and patience inherit what has been promised.

CHAPTER SIX

A BRIDGE FOR THE JOURNEY

HEBREWS 5:1-10; 7:1-28

Some journeys can't be completed without crossing the right bridge. That's why my wife and I have a photo of one sitting on our fireplace mantle. Decorating our home this way probably isn't going to get us on Martha Stewart's next special, but that's okay. This bridge has great practical and symbolic significance for our family. Therefore, the picture is right where it belongs.

The Confederation Bridge, you see, connects North America with Prince Edward Island, Canada. It is an engineering marvel. This structure, which is over 8 miles long, is designed to last 100 years. Go on the Confederation Bridge website and you can discover a number of fascinating details. If so inclined, you can purchase one of the official books that describe the building process and the challenges faced by the design and construction crews. You can discover that the main bridge piers are octagonal shafts and the girders range from 15 to 46 feet deep. You can read about the plethora of ways that people through history navigated their way from the mainland to P.E.I prior to the building of the bridge.

I may as well admit it up front, though. I really don't care about structural details. I'm no expert in bridge building; in fact, I'm poorly informed even for an amateur. Many of the details are simply beyond my mental grasp. I care about the Confederation Bridge for one reason: it gets me from New Brunswick to people that I care for deeply. Bridges, you see, do not simply connect land to land. They connect people, making face-to-face relationship possible.

Some journeys can't be completed without crossing the right bridge. That is why these chapters of Hebrews present God as the ultimate bridge builder. The goal of this divine construction project is the reconnecting of God and people. Understanding the need for and the nuances of this bridge-building activity requires a brief look back to the earliest chapters of Scripture.

In Genesis 1–2, Adam and Eve experienced the full fellowship with God that people were created to enjoy. With the entrance of sin into the world, however, a relational gap was created between God and people (Genesis 3). From that point forward a bridge was needed to span the distance between a glorious God and sin–stained people.

God took the initiative, reducing the gap by raising up a class of people called priests. These servants functioned as a relational go-between. This idea is captured in the imagery behind the term priest, which reflects the concept of bridge building. On the one hand, they represented the people before God. As God's appointed delegates, they presented sacrifices in behalf of the masses (Exod 28:38-44; Leviticus 1-6). On the other hand, they represented God before people. They helped people learn and apply God's truth (Deut 17:9; 19:17). On God's behalf, they pronounced his blessings upon the people (Num 6:23-26). By carrying out these (and many other) tasks, they helped people understand how God was at work in their lives. By representing God before people and vice versa, priests functioned as a human object lesson. They demonstrated that the gap between God and people was too great for humanity to cross on its own.

Within this process, an individual known as the high priest was especially prominent. He carried out a role in which even the other priests could not function. He would enter the Most Holy Place of the tabernacle, where God dwelt among his people, on the Day of Atonement (Leviticus 16). There the high priest would present sacrifices in order to maintain the people's relationship with God.

The high priest's role is the centerpiece of Hebrews 5–7. The location of the high priest's service and the specifics of what he did are the focus of Hebrews 8–10. These items are especially addressed in chapter nine of our study. Here in Hebrews 5–7, the emphasis is more on the office of high priest and the means by which the high priest was selected. According to Hebrews, this entire system was set up to help us understand the work of Jesus, who ultimately bridged the gap between us and God. If you want to understand what Jesus has done and is doing, says Hebrews, you've got to understand the role of a high priest.

> The entire Jewish system was set up to help us understand the work of Jesus, who ultimately bridged the gap between us and God.

Our study zeroes in on two passages that collectively prove the superiority of Jesus over high priests who functioned under the old covenant (5:1-10; 7:1-28). First, Jesus is compared with the levitical priesthood. This demonstrates that Jesus fulfilled certain prerequisites to high priesthood. Then, Jesus is contrasted with the old covenant priests to demonstrate his superiority over them.

Jesus Is Similar to Other High Priests (5:1-4)

At first glance, this material doesn't seem significant to us. It was very important for these Hebrew Christians, however. Their Jewish background had etched into their minds a deep awareness of the need for a God-sanctioned high priest. We need one every bit as badly—we just aren't as aware of it! These verses demonstrate that Jesus fits the bill.

First, Jesus and the old covenant priests shared a common *identity* (v. 1). That is to say, they were both human. At first this seems like an observation straight from the lips of Captain Obvious. What could possibly be more basic? This simple observation is crucial to the message of Hebrews, however. Because his job involved representing people before God the high priest had to be a human being. Under the old covenant an animal could function as sacrifice, but not sacrificer. Not made of the right stuff. Angels help God's people in many ways (1:14), but they couldn't function as high priests. Not made of the right stuff. In fact, God the Father couldn't even do so. Didn't have the right stuff. This explains, from the perspective of priesthood, why Jesus had to completely identify with humanity (Hebrews 2). The basic idea is the same, but the image used to describe it has shifted. Rather than describing Jesus as blazing a trail (2:10), these verses describe him as becoming a bridge. Doing so meant he had to have the right stuff.

Second, Jesus and the levitical priests both possessed a divine *commission* (vv. 1, 4). Under the old covenant, God had first selected Aaron, Moses' brother, as high priest (Exod 28–29). After Aaron died, God specifically demonstrated that the role was to be passed down through Aaron's descendants (Num 20:22ff). The point was powerfully and

‡

C
H
A
P
T
E
R

graphically established. Serving as high priest was the greatest honor an Israelite could experience (with the exception of Moses). Because of the role's symbolic significance, it was crucial that it be filled by divine appointment. The message of Scripture, therefore, was clear. The position could not be trained for, sought, or bought. Like all legitimate high priests, Jesus was appointed by God. He didn't seize the position; he was selected.

> The priesthood could not be trained for, sought, or bought. Jesus didn't seize the position; he was selected.

Third, Jesus and the old covenant high priests shared a common *function* (v. 1). The term *priest* is a function, not a title. Priests, by definition, do something. Therefore a priest that doesn't offer sacrifices, for example, is like a runner who doesn't run, a singer who doesn't sing, or a worker who doesn't work. Jesus did not simply have the designation "high priest" conferred upon him like an honorary degree. He offered sacrifice, just like any other priest (the nature of those sacrifices is emphasized in our study of Hebrews 9–10).

Finally, Jesus and levitical high priests needed to demonstrate a common *mentality* (v. 2). Priests had to deal gently with sin. The idea behind the Greek word is blurred somewhat by the NIV translation. The basic idea is that the high priest had to reflect a balanced and appropriate attitude toward sin/sinners. He had to mirror God's own heart so the people would have an accurate view of sin and God. For example, a high priest might function with an overly severe attitude toward worshipers, thereby denying them the sense of reconciliation to God. On the other hand, the high priest might function with a cavalier attitude toward the ritual. This would result in people not taking sin seriously. High priests could demonstrate this balance because they too were subject to temptation. As Hebrews demonstrates, Jesus was fully able to identify with us as well (2:17-18; 4:14-16).

These four elements of high priesthood are nonnegotiable items. By divine design, they were true of all high priests, regardless of when or under what covenant they functioned. They are provided to reinforce our confidence that Jesus truly fulfills God's intent for high priesthood when he created the office. For this to be true, however, Jesus also must clearly transcend the limitations of the former system. This is the primary emphasis of Hebrews 7, although it is implied in Hebrews 5:10.

Jesus Is Superior to Other High Priests (7:1-28)

The supremacy of Jesus' priesthood is demonstrated through a God-ordained analogy. On various occasions God used Old Testament figures, functions, furniture, and events to establish key concepts related to eventual New Testament truths. (The technical term for this is typology). In this instance, God raised up a priest named Melchizedek to demonstrate what Jesus' priesthood would be like. Outside of Hebrews 5–7, Melchizedek is only mentioned in Genesis 14:18-20 and Psalm 110:4. Since Hebrews alludes to the former and quotes the latter (twice), all biblical information on Melchizedek is used here. The parallels between Jesus and Melchizedek enable this obscure Old Testament figure to become a human illustration. Through this comparison, several superior components of Jesus' priesthood are evident.

First, Jesus' priesthood contains a greater *certainty*. This is demonstrated through a contrast between ways the priests demonstrated their legitimacy. Under the old covenant, a high priest proved his right to function through an appeal to his genealogy. He had to demonstrate that he was from the right branch of Aaron's family tree. Pedigree was of paramount importance.

> Jesus' priesthood contains a greater *certainty*.

Jesus, like Melchizedek, was not even from the tribe of Levi (7:3, 13-15). According to the old covenant, neither could function as a priest. One might assume the lack of levitical pedigree would make both Jesus and Melchizedek inferior. According to Hebrews, however, the opposite is true. In Melchizedek's case, the fact that he received the tithe from Levi's ancestor Abraham proved the priest was superior to all Abraham's descendants (vv. 4-10). While the logic of this seems rather complex to us, the point is that Melchizedek's lack of genealogy actually made him superior to the priestly tribe.

The same is true of Jesus, who descended from Judah. At this point, the writer of Hebrews makes a striking observation. Jesus' genealogy disqualified him from entering the part of the temple where priests served. Jesus facing restricted access to God? How can that possibly be? If God the Son faced restricted access to God the Father, it must say something about the entire priesthood under the old covenant!

Instead, Jesus' priesthood is verified by an oath from God (7:20-22). Whenever the Bible describes God taking an oath, something significant is always at stake. Here, God commits to Jesus that his priesthood will never end. Although the oath is given to Jesus, it is recorded for our sake. How do we know that God will never again change the high priesthood through which we gain access to him? Because God says "swear to God," that's why! God's character can already be trusted, since he does not lie (Titus 1:3). When God reinforces his promise with an oath, that's certainty wrapped in surety! God never made an oath regarding the levitical priesthood, because the entire system was designed to be temporary. Jesus' priesthood is guaranteed to endure, because God says so.

> God commits to Jesus that his priesthood will never end.

Furthermore, the certainty of Jesus' priesthood is guaranteed because of his resurrection (7:16, 23-24). Under the old covenant, people were consistently reminded that their priests faced the same mortality rate as everyone else. This was most poignantly demonstrated in the succession ceremony that took place upon Aaron's death (Numbers 20). According to Hebrews, Easter shows us that our high priest is alive! Though he died for us, he has also been raised for us. Therefore, he is able to eternally function as our representative in God's presence. There will never come a time when he will be unable, unwilling, or unqualified to intervene in our behalf.

> Jesus' priesthood is guaranteed because of his resurrection.

Second, Jesus' priesthood is characterized by an unparalleled *capability*. Hebrews highlights Jesus' connection to the tribe of Judah (7:14). This was Israel's royal line, from which kings came and the Messiah was anticipated. Because Jesus was from this tribe, he had the genealogical verification for a claim to kingship. When combined with the above material, we see that Jesus was qualified to function as a priest-king. Melchizedek also possessed this dual role, as one who symbolically pointed to Jesus. Again, the evidence for this gets a little complicated. Melchizedek's name/title is a Hebrew compound word, comprised of the terms "king" and "righteousness." Yet he was also a priest. Under the old covenant, this was not allowed. Levites were priests and not kings. Because Melchizedek lived prior to the old covenant, however, he was not bound by it. Similarly Jesus is both king (1:8-13) and priest, because he transcends the limitations of the old covenant.

This is great news for us! If Jesus were bound by the old covenant, a choice would have to be made. Either he could function as our ruling messianic king or he could function as our serving priest. We desperately need both. This is not a great time for an either/or proposition.

The genius of God is such that he planned a means by which he could meet both areas of our need through the only One fully capable of meeting either area of our need.

Jesus' priesthood is characterized by an unparalleled *morality*.

Third, Jesus' priesthood is characterized by an unparalleled *morality*. The portrait of Jesus as holy, blameless, pure, and set apart from sinners stresses the sinlessness of Jesus (7:26). Melchizedek's name symbolically illustrates this, since the last half of his name means "righteousness." Jesus, however, truly had no need to offer sacrifices for his own sin (7:27). In contrast, the levitical high priest had to offer sacrifices for his own sins before he could offer a sacrifice for anyone else (5:3). He was commanded to live a pure life (Mal 2:4-7), but inevitably fell short.

Jesus gives us the kind of high priesthood we desire and God requires. He does not simply represent us before God as one authentically human. He does so as one who lived up to God's intent for humanity (2:5-9). Jesus meets God's high standards regarding the purity of high priests. Furthermore, the quality of his character guarantees that he will approach the problem of sin with the balanced perspective God requires (5:2). As one completely pure, he always takes sin seriously. At the same time he demonstrates compassion to us strugglers. Such a high priest indeed meets our need (7:25)!

Jesus meets God's high standards regarding the purity of high priests.

This section of Hebrews proves some fairly detailed concepts through some fairly intricate argumentation. Perhaps you are a detail person—the kind who can't wait to read more about the specs on the Confederation Bridge. I hope you are even more consumed with learning the details of how God bridged the ultimate gap through our great high priest. Then again, maybe you are simply interested in the big picture and bottom line. If so, here you go.

First, these chapters remind us that God took the initiative to establish relationship with us. The priestly role was God's idea. Yes, virtually all religions have some kind of priesthood. The idea didn't start with people, though. It was established by God. Reading these chapters should fill us with wonder. God has always provided a means by which people could express relationship with him. Through Jesus, however, he has provided ultimate access.

Second, this material demonstrates Jesus is *the* bridge to God. All other persons or practices claiming such status are proved ineffective. Even the worship practices in Genesis through Malachi pointed forward to the superior blessings we have in Christ. As much as I love the Confederation Bridge, one can get to Prince Edward Island by ferry or plane. There is only one way from where we are to where God is. All other efforts, no matter how sincere, are futile.

> There is only one way from where we are to where God is.

Third, God has provided security in our relationship with him. Jesus is God's guarantee that the terms of his relational commitments to humanity will never change. There will never be another change in high priesthood. Jesus' appointment has no term limit. Therefore, we don't have to investigate every new (or other) religious system to see if it is God's "new thing." If Jesus tarries, our great grandchildren will be restored to God on the same terms and in the same way we were.

Fourth, God maintains ongoing relationship with us through Jesus' ministry. The same Jesus who prayed for his followers in John 17 continues his work in heaven (Rom 8:34; 1 John 2:1). Even now he stands as our representative before God the Father. Because of him, we can confidently approach God in prayer and worship (Heb 4:16).

Finally, Jesus' high priestly function means we need no other go-between in expressing our relationship with God. All Christians are now priests (1 Pet 2:5) with access to the presence of God through our high priest. Other believers who are especially committed, learned, or mature can greatly help us in our relationship with God. Besides Jesus, however, no one else is needed to gain access to God.

> Every bridge we see or cross should serve as a reminder of what Jesus has done and is doing for us.

In light of these truths, every bridge we see or cross should serve as a reminder of what Jesus has done and is doing for us. Maybe decorating the mantle with a bridge photo isn't such a bad idea. In fact, I got to looking a little closer at the fireplace in our living room. On the fireplace, we have a cross. On our hearth, we have an empty tomb. After reading Hebrews 5–7, those three things just seem to go together. Our living room seems more beautiful now. So does my journey through life. The right bridge sure makes a difference. Without him, the ultimate journey wouldn't be possible.

Activities for Your Group's Journey

1. What is your initial response to the detailed and sometimes intricate material in these chapters of Hebrews? Are you inclined toward researching specifics or getting to core issues? How is God prodding you to further growth as you strive to show commitment to him through your thinking (Matt 22:37)?

2. When you see or cross a bridge this week, use it as a memory trigger. Remind yourself that Jesus is continually interceding in behalf of you and others. Reflect on the practical difference this awareness made in your week. Was there a particular time or situation in which this knowledge especially encouraged you? If so, share your experience with the group.

3. Which of the unique elements of Jesus' high priesthood do you find most striking or meaningful? Why?

4. What are some ways that Christians live as if they need someone besides Jesus to provide them access to God? How about some ways Christians live as if they don't need anyone to provide them access to God?

5. How would your prayer life change if you fully realized the freedom of access to God that Jesus has made possible?

Memory Verse
Hebrews 7:23-25

Now there have been many of those priests, since death prevented them from continuing in office; [24]but because Jesus lives forever, he has a permanent priesthood. [25]Therefore he is able to save completely those who come to God through him, because he always lives to intercede for them.

CHAPTER SEVEN

PRIVILEGES FOR THE JOURNEY

HEBREWS 8:1-13

When you have an opportunity to travel in style, it is easy to take the privilege for granted. Perhaps you have experienced this yourself. It has come to have fresh meaning for me in just the past few days.

I'm finishing this chapter while on a trip with my family. Knowing the length of the journey, we decided to rent a car. When we arrived at the agency, however, no car was available in the class we had reserved. For a moment, I was concerned. Then, the manager began to speak. Everything seemed to move in slow motion as the words flowed from her lips. Beautiful words. Wonderful words. Words including the phrase "free upgrade." "Would we be interested?" she asked. "Let me think about it a moment," I replied. Francene and I stepped away from the counter for a moment of "consultation" (a mere formality). I answered in the affirmative, and soon was holding keys to a 2003 Cadillac DeVille. To put this in perspective, you need to know two things. First, we are on a *four week* trip. I'm driving a Caddy for a month! Second, our two cars are a Geo Prism (120,000+ miles) and a Chevy Lumina (170,000+ miles). An upgrade, indeed.

Do you remember Inspector Gadget trying to get a grip on his new-found accessories? That's what I must have looked like during my first few moments behind the wheel. (Our Prism is a bare bones model, even for a Prism!) I'm getting the hang of it, though. The individually adjustable seats and climate controls are tricky, but I'm learning. Cruise control, volume control, and selection control buttons clutter the steering wheel, but I'm managing. The smooth ride requires me to

58

monitor the speedometer a little more closely, but I'm adjusting. It has been a good week.

I'm also starting to think the car is a mixed blessing, though. The machine isn't giving me problems; I'm giving me problems. While becoming accustomed to privilege, I am also growing numb. With each passing day, I seem to have less awareness of just how good I have it. I'm already starting to sense a desire for something else, something different, something more. When one has an opportunity to travel in style, it is easy to take the privilege for granted.

> **When one has an opportunity to travel in style, it is easy to take the privilege for granted.**

Hebrews 8 is written to and for people who have joined the journey but have been jaundiced by a loss of perspective on their privileges. At first glance, these verses might not appear to offer much help. For starters, much of the chapter consists of a lengthy Old Testament quote (the longest in the New Testament, in fact). Such does not seem to be the stuff from which exciting Bible studies are created. Furthermore, both the writer of Hebrews and Jeremiah heavily emphasize the term covenant (it is used seven times in this chapter). Nothing gets a home group discussion flowing quite like technical theological jargon. Therefore, we might be tempted to bypass this chapter in pursuit of more "relevant" or "practical" material.

> **Careful consideration of Hebrews 8 can strengthen our appreciation for and our allegiance to the spiritual privileges Jesus makes available.**

In reality, these verses are a doctrinal and emotional apex within the book. Careful consideration of Hebrews 8 can strengthen our appreciation for and our allegiance to the spiritual privileges Jesus makes available. In order to grasp the impact of these verses, however, we need a basic understanding of the term covenant.

A covenant is essentially a binding relational agreement. Two biblical analogies may help clarify the picture. On the one hand, a covenant with God is like a marriage. This helps communicate the relational nature of biblical covenants. Our agreement with God is not coldly contractual. Therefore, the connection between God and Israel (under the old covenant) or the church (in the new covenant) is described via marriage imagery (Jer 2:2; Rev 19:7). On the other hand, our covenant with God is like a treaty between two unequal parties. For example, Deuteronomy is structured like an ancient treaty offered from a victorious nation to a vanquished people. This balances the marriage imagery; our covenant with God is relational, but not level. He sets the terms of the deal. We are free to accept or reject, but we cannot negotiate.

Hebrews 8 reminds believers that the new covenant forms the basis upon which God relates to people. It is not *a* way of relating to God; it is *the* way of relating to God. The believers receiving this letter were tempted to revert from Christianity to Judaism. Doing so would not merely be refusing a free upgrade in their relationship with God—it would be voiding their relationship with God. The two covenants do not coexist. The new supersedes the old. There is a lesson here for us, even if conversion to Judaism doesn't tempt us. It is not enough for people to be "spiritual." A right relationship with God requires an acceptance of the terms he offers. This in turn requires embracing Jesus—the one through whom God put the new covenant into effect. Let's take this opportunity to wallow in the blessings God has made available through Christ (8:6). Doing so will help us appreciate the journey and will strengthen our resolve to remain on the right path.

> Let's take this opportunity to wallow in the blessings God has made available through Christ.

We Receive a Superior Transformation by God (8:10)

One new covenant hallmark is the inner change experienced by those who are part of it. In every era of God's relationships with people, he has been concerned about the softness of people's hearts toward him. During the old covenant, for example, he did not simply want robotic obedience. Israelites were commanded to internalize God's truth (Deut 6:6) and circumcise their hearts (Deut 10:11), which required committing the inner person to God. By such heartfelt obedience, they could demonstrate gratitude to God for his gracious offer of covenant relationship. In fact, God himself promised to partner with them so they could demonstrate this allegiance (Deut 30:9).

During the old covenant, however, the way God partnered with people was different. As symbolized by the tablets on which the Ten Commandments were written, God's laws began their transforming work outside the person (Exod 24:12; 34:1). They were designed, as it were, to work their way in from the outside. The problem, however, was the condition of the human heart. It proved resistant to God's transforming influence (Heb 3:12; 8:8-9). This arrangement between God and people demonstrated that, in the words of Seth Wilson, Dean Emeritus of Ozark Christian College, "people need a new heart, not a new start."

> **God transforms us from the inside by giving us the spiritual equivalent of a heart transplant.**

This is precisely what God has provided in our relational agreement with him. He transforms us from the inside by giving us the spiritual equivalent of a heart transplant. This inside-out work of God is reflected through the imagery of God's laws being written on our hearts and minds (8:10). God's graffiti is written via the work of the Holy Spirit inside us (2 Cor 3:3). As a result, our desires are progressively transformed so we want to know and obey God's truth. This sacred surgery transforms our affections and allegiances.

I recently observed the power of a new affection while attending a basketball game. As the game progressed, I became more fascinated with the crowd and less focused on the players. My attention zeroed in on one young lady in particular. I know this young woman pretty well—well enough to know she is not interested in sports. On this particular day, however, she was obviously elated to be watching hoops. The reason quickly became evident. She was not focused on hoops, but on a particular hoopster. She was soon counting points, assists, rebounds, and fouls—when they related directly to the object of her affection. For her, attending basketball games had suddenly been transformed from a have-to into a get-to. That is what the Holy Spirit does for us. He produces an intrinsic motivation for godly living by transforming us at the level of our basic desires. As a result, living out God's desire for our lives is increasingly recognized for what it truly is—a joy rather than an obligation.

> **Living out God's desire for our lives is increasingly recognized for what it truly is—a joy rather than an obligation.**

This verse is not teaching us to simply "follow our hearts" when making choices, however. The Holy Spirit's presence in our lives does not guarantee perfect harmony between God's desires and our own. Our choices are still subject to Scripture's scrutiny (Heb 4:12-13). Following our hearts breaks the hearts of God and people when doing so leads us in inappropriate and irresponsible directions. Therefore, even the most mature Christian cannot follow his or her inclinations *carte blanche*. By the same token, this verse shows that our conversion to Christ produces a change in our basic orientation toward the things of God. God's supernatural power should make us increasingly inclined toward his ways.

We Receive a Superior Knowledge of God (8:11)

A second gift from God is the universal opportunity for people to know him directly and deeply. During the old covenant era, a hierarchy existed within Israel. Three classes of individuals were commissioned and empowered by God for leadership among the people. Those three groups were prophets, priests, and kings. The Holy Spirit empowered them for spiritual service, and, at their best, each group partnered with God in nurturing the spiritual development of Israel.

In the new covenant God directly teaches all believers through the Holy Spirit's residing within. As a result, Christians are enabled to enjoy an experiential relationship with God that transcends opportunities made available by the former covenant. The Holy Spirit progressively cultivates a close connection between God and us.

This past February, Francene and I attended a Valentine's Day dinner at an area church. The program included a scaled-down version of the newlywed game. Every couple participated and the results were humorous, but predictable. Most couples got about half the questions correct. Then a special couple came forward for their turn. Lord willing, they will celebrate seventy years of marriage next year! I'm glad the newlywed game wasn't designed as a one-on-one single elimination tournament. None of the rest of us would have had any chance at the free coffee mugs! They answered the questions effortlessly. Oh, they were polite about it. It was pretty obvious that they didn't find the game especially challenging, however. When two people are bonded together for that long, I guess they sort of get to know one another.

The Holy Spirit provides *each* Christian the potential for that kind of relationship with God. Of course length of relationship doesn't guarantee depth of relationship—with God or others. When we actively partner with the Holy Spirit, however, an accurate, increasing knowledge of God is the result.

‡

C
H
A
P
T
E
R

Of course length of relationship doesn't guarantee depth of relationship—with God or others.

By the way, this privilege does not negate our need to receive effective preaching and teaching from other Christians. While the Holy Spirit is our ultimate teacher, he also works through the insights of others. In fact, he equips particular individuals with the ability to strengthen the church through preaching and teaching (Eph 4:11-13). Thus, he works on both the "giving" and "receiving" end of the process. Christians sometimes attempt to use this verse as an exemption clause freeing them from the need for "human" teachers. Doing so reflects a misunderstanding of how the Holy Spirit accomplishes his teaching ministry.

We Receive a Superior Reconciliation to God (8:12)

A third privilege in our covenant relationship with God is the full and final forgiveness of sin. This blessing receives the heaviest emphasis in Hebrews generally and chapters 8–10 specifically. Our next lesson directly addresses how sin was dealt with in the old covenant compared to the new. Therefore, attention here is focused specifically on the last part of verse twelve, which is frequently misunderstood.

Songs, skits, and sermons often use this verse to teach that God no longer recalls the sins of the forgiven believer. It is as if God, who knows everything, has deleted this information from his memory bank. Throughout the Bible, however, God's followers are commanded by God's messengers to repent. How can God command repentance from sins he doesn't remember? Furthermore, in spite of popular opinion to the contrary, God doesn't even want *us* to *completely* forget our past. The apostle Paul, for example, actually challenges believers to remember what they were outside of Christ (Eph 2:11-13; Titus 2:3). Some counselor Paul would make! He recognized, however, that forgetting how bad things were keeps us from appreciating how good things are.

> Forgetting how bad things were keeps us from appreciating how good things are.

How good *do* we have it, then? What does Jeremiah mean when he anticipates an era of "forgotten" sin? The idea must be understood legally, not literally. The terms *forgiveness* (in the first part of 8:12) and *remember* (in the last part of verse 12) are essentially synonyms. Our sin is not a barrier in the forefront of God's mind, separating him from the Christian. When God considers our sin, so to speak, he does not just see our sin. He sees Jesus' payment for our sin. Because the debt has been paid, the debt is "forgotten."

Our everyday conversation contains similar uses of these terms. A few days ago, one of my children broke a coffee carafe. We are staying in another couple's home, so the event was especially traumatic. My response to the situation was, "We'll forget about that." I did not mean the situation would go unresolved, nor was I anticipating an instantaneous amnesia attack. I was freeing my child to enjoy our trip by saying, "I'll pay for your mistake." Through Jesus, God has done the same for us.

Throughout history, God has offered people a relationship with himself through the establishing of covenants. While each was an undeserved gift, not all gifts are created equal. Writing under the old covenant, Jeremiah anticipated a better arrangement. Joining his voice with God's, Jeremiah cried out "the time is coming" (Heb 8:7). Joining his voice with God's, the writer of Hebrews cries out, "the time is now" (Heb 8:6). Now is the time to join our voices in gratitude for these spiritual blessings. Let's avoid taking them for granted. Through Jesus, we are not merely enabled to complete the journey. We are equipped to do so in style!

Activities for Your Group's Journey

1. "Traveling in style" can make people arrogant. How do we acknowledge and appreciate our spiritual blessings without acting as if we are better than everyone else? Furthermore, Hebrews 8 has sometimes been used to justify persecution of Jews. Nazi workers at Auschwitz, for example, celebrated Christmas and Easter. How can Christians respect Jews while still affirming the message of Hebrews 8?

2. What are some benefits of using the marriage analogy as a way to understand our relationship with God? How does this picture change the way you think about prayer? Bible study? Obedience? Disobedience? What are some potential dangers in thinking about our relationship with God this way?

3. Hebrews 6:13–8:13 uses several legal terms to help us understand our relationship with God (swear, oath, confirms, law, regulation, set aside, guarantee, covenant, mediator, founded, and obsolete are all examples). What are some benefits of using legal imagery as a way to understand our relationship with God? How does this picture change the way you think about the items mentioned in question 2? What are some potential dangers in thinking about our relationship with God this way?

4. Do you tend to rely too much on the spiritual insights of others? Or do you tend to undervalue the insights of others? How do we balance this delicate issue?

5. In your group prayer time, focus specifically on thanking God for our spiritual privileges. Feel free to share prayer concerns, but pray about them as individuals between meetings. This is a time to wallow together in the goodness of God. Rejoice together in his blessings.

Memory Verse
Hebrews 8:10-12

"This is the covenant I will make with the house of Israel after that time," declares the Lord. "I will put my laws in their minds and write them on their hearts. I will be their God, and they will be my people. ¹¹No longer will a man teach his neighbor, or a man his brother, saying, 'Know the Lord,' because they will all know me, from the least of them to the greatest. ¹²For I will forgive their wickedness and will remember their sins no more."

CHAPTER EIGHT

CLEANSING FOR THE JOURNEY

HEBREWS 9:1–10:18

There's no feeling in the world quite like the feeling of clean. I am reminded of this every summer when we go camping. On the surface, it is merely a getaway. You know the deal. Beanie weenies, smores, morning hikes, afternoons in the hammock, evenings by the fire . . . the typical family camp-out. In reality, however, these outings are a spiritual retreat and summer revival. For the rest of the clan, rejuvenation comes from getting close to the earth. They love nature—both animate and inanimate. For me, revival comes from letting the earth get close to me. Camping allows me to get dirty. Really dirty. There's no dirty quite like been-camping-for-a-week-and-I-can't-get-it-off-me-dirty. Sure, we pitch our tent in campgrounds with shower facilities. We even use them occasionally. When tent camping, however, you never emerge from a bath clean. You just come out a different kind of dirty. Therefore, the ride home never smells quite as pleasant as the drive to the campsite.

Actually, I relish the experience. Here's why. When you forget how gross it feels to be grimy, you forget how good it feels to be clean. I love camping out because I love cleaning up. (You've been there, even if you aren't a nature buff. Everyone knows a bath after mowing in July, for example, is different than one after Jenga in January—unless you really get into playing Jenga). Therefore, after unloading, I undergo the hour of shower. I shampoo twice. If the monthly bills are paid, I shampoo three times. I use both liquid and bar soap. I stay in until the hot water is gone, dry off with a towel that doesn't smell like smoke, and put on something freshly laundered. Then, I meditate on how good it feels to be clean. Once in a while, I even open my Bible to Hebrews 9–10. These chapters speak volumes to people who want to feel refreshed.

Something within us yearns for freedom from filth.

Something within us, you see, yearns for freedom from filth. What we need, however, transcends the best baths. The worst muck, moral and spiritual failure, is found deep within. We are soiled and struggle to solve it. Therefore we get frustrated with ourselves, exasperated with others, and grumpy with God. Because we can't get the dirt off, our outlook on everything and everyone is impacted. If we want to travel well, then, we've got to travel clean.

In the Old Testament era, a variety of regulations and rituals helped a person maintain clean status (see Leviticus 11–17). Through washings, offerings, and sacrifices people strove to sustain the ceremonial purity necessary for right relationships with God and people. The ultimate cleansing ceremony, however, occurred on the Day of Atonement (see Leviticus 16). On this one day, the high priest entered an otherwise prohibited section of Israel's worship center (for more details on this tabernacle, see Heb 9:1-10). Known as the Most Holy place, it was the location where God's presence appeared among Israel. There, the high priest presented animal blood to purify the people.

This yearly cleansing process provides the framework necessary to understand Hebrews 9:1–10:18. The figures, furniture, and functions associated with the former system are an analogy pointing to Jesus (9:1-10). When he died in our place, purity became possible. His blood washes away the stains of sin.

What a profound paradox. Experience tells us virtually nothing stains worse than blood. The Bible, however, tells us that only Jesus' blood can remove sin's stains. Some detergent. Therefore, be advised: the following pages may produce squeamishness. There's no way to address this topic without thinking about blood. When we do, bear this in mind. When you read about blood in Hebrews 9–10, remember it is an image for death. There wasn't something magical about Jesus' blood; it wasn't that a finger prick resulting in a few drops could remove our sin. He had to die. These verses describe four differences his self-sacrifice makes in believers' lives. Each is introduced in 9:11-12 and developed in following verses.

Cleansing for the Journey

Jesus' Blood Gives Us Cleansing (9:13-14, 22)

God used the Day of Atonement as one way (among many) to teach spiritual lessons. It showed the penalty for sin is death (Rom 6:23) and that God accepts an approved substitute in the sinners' place. A bull and goat were offered on this special day, but they paled in comparison to Jesus. Two interrelated reasons show why.

First, Jesus possesses better *quality*. Sacrificial animals had to be free of physical blemish (Lev 14:10; Num 6:14; 19:2), but Jesus was free of moral blemish. The Holy Spirit helped Jesus live perfectly so he could fulfill this requirement. Animals cannot possess moral blamelessness; they don't make ethical decisions. They cannot fully represent a person either since they aren't one. The only truly effective sacrifice had to be completely pure and completely human. Jesus alone filled the bill.

> The only truly effective sacrifice had to be completely pure and completely human. Jesus alone filled the bill.

Therefore, Jesus provides better *cleansing*. The rituals associated with the former system only addressed the outer person. Since bulls and goats lacked moral purity, they couldn't cleanse people on the inside where choices are determined (Matt 15:1-20). Because Jesus lived wholly holy, he can clean us to the core.

My first car was a 1978 Cutlass. Francene and I went on high school dates in this car. I went to college in this car. We went on our honeymoon in this car. Our first child was brought home from the hospital in this car. It even showed up in the videos when the next two children were brought home. I usually don't get attached to machinery, but this car belongs in the Smithsonian.

One summer evening we had just finished a baked chicken dinner. Since we disposed of our trash elsewhere, Francene bagged the leftover gook and put it in the car. Unfortunately, the windows were left down. Did I mention we lived in rural Joplin, Missouri? The next morning raccoon tracks were on the hood. Gristle and grease were ground into the cloth seats. Foul thoughts ran through my mind. That's no way to travel.

Fortunately, I was well supplied. Dad owned an auto supply store. I started by cleaning the vinyl cracks in the roof. I had a good toothbrush and industrial strength cleaner. The roof looked swell, but oh the smell. So I washed the car, using official auto supply store soap. I even dried with a chamois. Nobody uses a chamois, but I did. The hood looked swell, but oh the smell. Next I waxed the car, giving detailed attention to the bumpers and chrome trim. The trim looked swell, but oh the smell. I even scrubbed the tires with whitewall cleaner. The tires looked swell . . . you get the point.

Ridiculous isn't it? Internal stench isn't solved by external solutions. Yet, the old covenant system could do nothing more and neither can our best efforts. I doubt anyone was tempted to slaughter an animal before opening prayer at your last group meeting. (If so, I sincerely hope your group doesn't eat refreshments first). We sometimes try to cover up our inner filth through religious rituals, however. These verses remind us we can't sing, fast, or give our way clean. Attendance pins and committee memberships won't get the job done either. Only the blood of Jesus can and does.

Jesus' Blood Gives Us a Covenant (9:15-21)

Jesus' sacrifice is also superior because it secures a better contract between us and God. Hebrews 9:15 describes Jesus as our mediator. The idea is similar to the trailblazing (Hebrews 2) and bridge-building concepts (Hebrews 7), except here courtroom language is used. Jesus stands between God and people, bringing both parties together in legally binding relationship. Putting the covenant into effect required bloodshed, due to the sin that separates God and people. Just like a will isn't binding until the testator dies (vv. 16-17), the covenant offered by God didn't take effect until the death of Jesus, who makes it possible.

The ceremony establishing the old covenant illustrated the relationship between ratification and sacrificial death (Exodus 24). When the Israelites entered this binding relationship with God, Moses took blood from animal sacrifices and sprinkled it over the entire assembly. As he did so, he told them, "This is the blood of the covenant" (Exod 24:8).

The Israelites were sprinkled with animal blood so they could be ceremonially qualified for covenant relationship with God. Our entrance into a committed relationship with God occurs when we are sprinkled with the blood of Jesus (Heb 9:15; 10:22). Jesus himself indicated the former was an illustration pointing toward the latter. When he established the significance of the cup in the Lord's Supper, he echoed Moses' words (Matt 26:28). Once cleansed through his death, we are qualified to receive the blessings promised to God's covenant people.

The story is told of a beggar who began to weep uncontrollably when informed of John Rockefeller's death. A man standing nearby was surprised by this and asked, "Why are you upset? Were you related to him?" "No," replied the poor man, "That's why I am crying." This doesn't have to be our story. Jesus is heir of all the Father possesses. Our trust in his sacrifice makes us siblings. Because we are his family, the blessings of Hebrews 8 are our birthright. Make no mistake about it, however. The privileges do not come cheaply. They cost Jesus his life.

Jesus' Blood Gives Us Clearance (9:24-25)

Jesus' sacrifice is also superior because it is presented in a better place. God was present in the Most Holy Place on the Day of Atonement, but he transcends cubic footage. Therefore the high priest was only with God to a limited extent. Jesus, however, has entered the fullness of God's presence to present his sacrifice (9:12). By doing so, Jesus fulfilled both roles in the Day of Atonement ritual. He is both supreme sacrifice and perfect priest.

Jesus is both supreme sacrifice and perfect priest.

Furthermore, his blood purified God's presence so we could enter it. As flawed people, high priests under the old system had to sprinkle blood in the Most Holy Place before offering sacrifices. Their sin contaminated the room. Similarly, God's full presence needed cleansing before we could gain access. God's presence was pure, but our presence there would contaminate it. Therefore, Jesus purified God's presence for us and us for God's presence. We have access to the throne room of heaven because Jesus makes us clean.

Have you ever faced restricted access to a place you really wanted to enter? Perhaps you have stood outside the player's entrance at a baseball park and strained your neck trying to see past the "Players Only" sign. Maybe you've tried to distract the executive secretary with a diversion so you could sneak in and put your feet on the boss's desk. Restricted access creates its own special brand of longing. This is what all Israelites except the high priest experienced regarding the Most Holy Place. It essentially contained a sign saying "Access Denied." Jesus didn't just change the sign. He put into effect a whole relationship with God.

Jesus' Blood Gives Us Confidence (9:27–10:18)

Jesus' sacrifice is also superior because it lasts. This is also shown by a contrast with the Day of Atonement ritual, which occurred every year. On the surface, it might seem like the frequency would reinforce people's confidence in their relationship with God. In reality, the regularity magnified a sense of guilt. The constant sacrifices reminded people their sin was continually being covered. God's acceptance of the offering gave people awareness that their sin had been temporarily addressed. They did have a certain sense of forgiveness rather than futility. What they lacked was a sense of finality.

> **Jesus' death was a single event with enduring effectiveness.**

In contrast, Jesus' death was a single event with enduring effectiveness. In reality, he couldn't die more than once anyhow. As one fully human, he possessed the same mortality ratio as anyone else— once per person. That one death atoned for all sin, including sin committed prior to his earthly life (9:15). Therefore, there is a huge difference between what Christians do during the Lord's Supper and what Israelites did on the Day of Atonement. We are not consuming emblems in the hope God will provide reconciliation to himself. We are celebrating the certainty that he has done so.

As a result, we are set free from the nagging and gnawing sense of guilt we carry because of our sin (10:2). By this, the text does not mean Christians should never feel guilty about anything. Sometimes our sense of guilt results from legitimate conviction, fueled by the Holy Spirit's training of our conscience. The text is saying our consciousness of sin doesn't have to be a barrier separating us from God. At the same time, a right relationship with God does help us deal with guilty feelings in productive and restoring ways. Knowing God has forgiven us can help us forgive ourselves.

That's why we have to talk about blood in church. I know some people find the whole discussion rather primitive. It is certainly a little gory when you stop to think about it. We come to worship looking our best. We shower and shave. We put on our best clothing (or our least wrinkled clothing). We wash our cars and shine our shoes. We bring a pleasant demeanor and dignified presence. We are, generally speaking, a good-looking bunch. Then we sing songs about blood. We hear Scriptures that talk about blood. We gather before a table with a cup representing blood. We see symbols of shed blood in the form of a cross. It seems we can't experience a worship service without repeatedly encountering a subject too grotesque for polite conversation. Maybe that's the irony of it all. We clean ourselves up so we can celebrate a purification we couldn't produce. So we talk, sing, and think about blood. We must. Until we are willing to do so, we don't have anything else to talk, sing, or think about. On the Christian journey, there's nothing quite like the feeling of traveling clean. In fact, it is the only way we can make the trip at all. 🔲

✠

C
H
A
P
T
E
R

8   *Cleansing for the Journey*

Activities for Your Group's Journey

1. This chapter describes four effects of Jesus' death in our behalf. Which of the four is the most meaningful to you on this particular day? Why?

2. If someone in the group has watched or participated in killing and butchering an animal, have them describe the process. It is certainly multisensory, to say the least! How do you think you would have felt as an active participant in the sacrifices offered under the old covenant? How does recognizing the gory nature of such sacrifices provide fresh perspective on the death of Jesus for you?

3. Make a list of songs (contemporary or traditional) in which the lyrics address the topic of blood. Jot down the specific lines of the song if you can remember them. Have some group members read the specific lines aloud. Reflect on the apparent absurdity of these lines to those outside the faith. You might even ask a non-Christian or older child what their gut-level response is to the lyrics.

4. Close the meeting by celebrating the Lord's Supper together. As you do so, reflect on how good it feels to be made clean.

Memory Verse Hebrews 9:27-28

Just as man is destined to die once, and after that to face judgment, [28]so Christ was sacrificed once to take away the sins of many people; and he will appear a second time, not to bear sin, but to bring salvation to those who are waiting for him.

CHAPTER NINE

CHECKPOINTS ON THE JOURNEY

HEBREWS 10:19-25

It's confession time: I have a compulsive need to monitor my progress. I don't keep a to-do list primarily for the sake of memory recall; I make one for the satisfaction of being able to check things off the list. I still use a paper planner rather than a PDA, and one sublime joy of being technologically challenged is the feel of pen on paper when the check mark is made. If the day is especially unproductive, I'm sometimes tempted to pad the list just to create a comforting illusion (breathe, eat, blink, sleep . . . you get the picture). On such days I also make the check mark very slowly, just to massage the moment. I know, I know . . . I'm sick; but, some of you can relate better than you want to admit!

This compulsion carries over to my journeys. For example, I'm one of the few people who actually looks at those airline magazines. I don't read the articles (does anybody?), but I do look at the route map periodically. Even when I cannot see the ground below, I like glancing at my watch and attempting to gauge my progress.

Most people who hike treat the scenic vistas as an opportunity to appreciate God's creation from a different vantage point. I look down, look up, chart past performance, and project the estimated time of arrival.

On car trips, I sometimes keep the map out even if know the route. Just like to monitor things. This past summer our family took a 2200 mile van ride (one way). My son asked to borrow the map. He sought our current coordinates, determined the approximate percentage of the trip completed, and charted our progress city by city. Afraid my wife would notice, I covered my involuntary smile of satisfaction. Later on, however, I pulled him aside and encouraged him. Like father, like son.

Here's the thing, though. Monitoring progress is fundamentally a good idea, especially on a journey as important as this one. Just because a few of us get carried away doesn't mean the idea should be ignored. Otherwise, it is hard to tell that you are off course. Checkpoints are kind of the traveler's equivalent of a check mark, so let's consider a few. We are approaching a good resting point in our journey through Hebrews, so take advantage of the opportunity, savor the process, and resist the temptation to rush forward.

> **Checkpoints are kind of the traveler's equivalent of a check mark.**

Hebrews 10:19-25 functions like a checkpoint in relationship to the whole letter. The material both summarizes the major emphases in the first ten chapters and anticipates subjects awaiting fuller attention. It is perhaps the best single passage for consideration of Hebrews in a microcosm. The reason is simple: in this one passage, which is a single sentence in the original language of the New Testament, the writer summarizes both what Jesus has done (the "doctrinal" core of the book), and how we should respond (the "practical" core of the book). The breadth and balance of the passage make it an appropriate stopping-off point on our journey through Hebrews.

Here is the goal, then, for the study of this chapter. Take some time, both individually and collectively, to reflect on your journey thus far. Do so from two different perspectives; first, from the vantage point of your overall lifelong journey with Christ and second, from the vantage point of your study through the book of Hebrews as a part of this particular study group. At times, this may feel like a review session. That's okay. Review is part of what this passage is designed to accomplish.

Doctrinal Checkpoints

Hebrews 10:19 reminds us that Jesus' priesthood enables both him and us to enter a superior location—the fullness of God's presence (the true Most Holy Place). This idea has been especially developed in the previous few chapters (8:1-6; 9:1-12, 24-25). We can do so, because Jesus has offered a sacrifice of superior blood—his own, not that of bulls or goats (9:11ff).

Hebrews 10:20 stresses the same truth through a slightly different image (echoing the message of 10:8-18). Because Jesus died a literal bodily death, he provides an access to God that was denied under the old covenant (as symbolized in the veil between the Holy Place and Most Holy Place of the tabernacle). After Jesus' death, the veil was torn, graphically and literally demonstrating this truth (Matt 27:51). The veil was torn from top to bottom, an object lesson showing that this was due to God's work and not our own. Jesus' body, says Hebrews, became the bridge crossing the chasm between the Holy and Most Holy Place.

> Jesus' body became the bridge crossing the chasm between the Holy and Most Holy Place.

The following verse brings to mind themes that were introduced much earlier in Hebrews. Much of the book revolves around Jesus' high priesthood; the designation of Jesus as *great* priest most specifically echoes 4:14 and also reintroduces the material in 2:17-18 and 3:1-6. The connection to chapter three is especially made clear through the reference to God's people as a house. Through architectural imagery, Hebrews describes Christians as individual parts that are collectively shaped into a dwelling place belonging to God in which his Spirit dwells (cf. 1 Cor 6:19; 1 Pet 2:4-5).

Practical Checkpoints

This portion is really the central thrust of the passage. Having been reminded of what Jesus has done, we are now challenged to respond appropriately. Hebrews 10:22-25 contains three separate commands that those who have embraced Jesus are challenged to obey.

First, we are to *embrace God's invitation to intimacy* (v. 22). This command is presented via some rather technical sounding language—that of drawing near to God. The word that is translated "draw near" is used in a variety of contexts to describe people gaining access to God. It was used in the Old Testament to describe what the high priest did on the Day of Atonement when he would enter the Most Holy Place of the tabernacle. It is used in Hebrews six times outside this verse, though it is sometimes translated differently into English (4:16; 7:25; 10:1; 11:6; 12:18, 22). Hebrews is saying that Jesus has died to provide us access to God, and we are expected to avail ourselves of the opportunity. This is an invitation because it is at God's initiative, but it is also an invitation we are commanded to accept. This command isn't about God forcing himself upon us, however. He isn't an insecure, unlovable King who tries to legislate his way into friendship and popularity. He issues the command; we are free to choose the response. Its just that choosing against God results in missing out on the wonder of all you were created to know, experience, and be.

Perhaps you, like me, are an Abraham Lincoln fan. My favorite Lincoln story occurred during the Civil War. The President was involved in a top-secret meeting with his closest advisors. During such meetings nobody was supposed to enter the War Room unless it was an absolute emergency. It was quite a surprise, therefore, when the door to the room swung open and a twelve-year-old boy entered. Not satisfied with this level of intrusion, the young man marched in a beeline to the front of the room. There, he proceeded to confidently place himself on the lap of the President of the United States of America. Sounds pretty presumptuous, huh? Perhaps it makes a difference when you realize the boy's name was Todd; as in, Todd Lincoln.

> **God has an entire universe to run,**
> **yet he has time for you, his child.**

Hebrews is saying there is a sense in which you can do that with God. He has an entire universe to run, yet he has time for you, his child. The price of such access is high, but he has long since arranged for the price to be paid. That's the message of Hebrews. We do have to respond on his terms, however, and the text addresses a few of them.

Access to God requires a sincere heart. The term *sincere* basically means authentic. It is used elsewhere in Hebrews 8:2 and 9:24 with reference to the "true" tabernacle. The term "heart" is addressing more than our emotions. In the first-century world, the heart was a metaphor for the inner core of a person—the essence of what defines you as you. This includes the will and the mind.

Access to God requires inward cleansing. This idea is captured through the *sprinkling* language of verse 22. The writer of Hebrews is referring back to Hebrews 9:16-22 and ultimately to Exodus 24:8. Just as those under the old covenant were literally sprinkled with blood to show their acceptance of a committed relationship with God, those under the new covenant are described as being inwardly "sprinkled" with the blood of Jesus. This is simply a way of saying that we have embraced the sacrifice of Jesus for our sins; therefore, the significance of his death is an effective reality in our lives.

Access to God requires outward cleansing. This is indicated by the *washing* terminology of verse 22. Jews practiced washing rituals designed to produce outward cleansing (perhaps Numbers 19 is most directly in view). The imagery of this verse points toward baptism as the corresponding New Testament practice. The basic idea is that baptism is an outward cleansing that symbolically parallels the inward cleansing mentioned above.

Are you embracing his invitation? Will you? Simply lingering at this checkpoint for a moment and realizing the implications of this opportunity could transform your prayer life more than a thousand seminars. It could reinvigorate your worship more than a thousand songs. It could jump-start your Bible study more than a thousand sermons. Will it?

The second major command is in 10:23. We are to *embrace God's plea for perseverance*. This one verse beautifully captures both our responsibility and God's role in the Christian journey.

Our responsibility is captured in the term translated "hold unswervingly" by the NIV (this same word was used in Heb 3:6). The importance of our grasp is graphically portrayed in the imagery behind this word.

I have a friend in the northeastern U.S. who recently experienced the essence of this idea. His family was hosting some friends for a visit, and they decided to take a hike together. The journey took them through something that in the northeast is known as a "waterfall." (I live in the Midwest. We would consider it water experiencing a slight descent after flowing over rocks—though most people wouldn't put it quite that way). They needed to climb down the "waterfall," so my friend went first. Their visitors have a preschool daughter, and decided to hand their child down to him. When he grabbed her, the balance of weight was thrown off and he slipped. Falling backward into the torrent, he clutched the child to his chest, rotated (unintentionally), and fell *on* her. As they began to float downstream, he rolled over and lifted the child out of the water. Although a thousand thoughts go through a person's mind at a time like that, he says a single thought blocked out all others. ***Whatever happens, don't let go of this child!*** The story has a happy ending. Everything turned out fine. The real question is, how will everything turn out for you? Put yourself in my friend's position for a moment. Imagine yourself in a rushing river with the strength of your grasp determining someone else's safety. Can you feel your hands beginning to cramp? Can you see your knuckles turning white? That is the tone and texture of this word. The verse is saying that kind of tenacity should characterize the way we hold to our hope in Christ. Some things are too precious to risk letting go.

Some things are too precious to risk letting go.

Checkpoints on the Journey

Of course, our rescue is not *merely* determined by our own effort. We are motivated to hold firmly based on our confidence in God's faithfulness. Hebrews 6:13-20 reminds us that we can trust God to keep his promises. The same idea resurfaces here. The trustworthiness of God directly impacts the tenacity of our grasp, because resolve is strengthened when we know our holding on makes a difference. We can hold firmly to our end of the rescue rope, as it were, because we are absolutely certain God will not let go of his end.

So, here's the question as we pause at this checkpoint. How's your grip? We have every confidence on the authority of Scripture that God is holding on. What about you?

The third major command is to *embrace God's challenge to community* (10:24-25). At first glance, it looks as if verse 24 and verse 25 are separate commands. The grammatical structure of these verses demonstrates, however, that the command in the text is actually to spur one another on toward love and good deeds (v. 24). Assembling together (v. 25) is a means by which we can make that happen.

Spurring one another implies a willingness to challenge one another on the journey. The term is a strong word that is often used negatively (see Acts 15:39), but not here. Sometimes a fellow traveler needs a hug; sometimes a pilgrim needs a kick in the kicking spot. The challenge to community requires both exhortation and encouragement. It also involves the willingness to both give and receive.

If we never spend time life-on-life, neither will happen. Therefore, the writer of Hebrews challenges us to regularly assemble while we await the end of our journey and the return of our king. The word for "assemble" came to signify the Sunday worship assembly, so this is what Hebrews especially has in view. (The material is easily applicable to small groups as well, however.) We tend to emphasize that the worship assembly is for an audience of One; in so doing, we run the risk of making our gathering entirely vertical in orientation. Hebrews reminds us, however, that one way we please our audience of One is by authentically and meaningfully helping one another on the road to maturity.

One way we please our audience of One
is by helping one another.

Here's a representative example of how these verses can be applied. Sometimes it seems as if worship assemblies and small groups are the hardest place to talk about God. If you are inclined to question this, think about the casual conversations that take place before and after our services, classes, meals, and meetings. In many instances, the conversations center around "small talk" that is not noticeably different from what takes place every day in checkout lines, around water fountains, on playgrounds, and in parking lots. We talk about the weather, sports, current events, family, and friends. Did I mention the weather? You can create plenty of elbow room at the next church social event by asking people direct questions about their relationship with God.

> One thing is for sure. Nothing is going to happen
> if we fail to get within spurring distance of one another.

Hebrews challenges us to transform our "small talk" into "big talk." Yes, this can be taken too far. No, I don't always appreciate having a total stranger or mild acquaintance directly confront me regarding my eternal destiny while I am standing in the Krispy Kreme line or watching Jim Edmonds bat. Such "spurring" happens best (and most redemptively) in the safe haven of unconditional covenant friendships. On the other hand, the deepest and most authentic relationships cannot form until we are willing to risk talking about matters that matter most. One thing is for sure. Nothing is going to happen if we fail to get within spurring distance of one another. Come to think of it, another thing is for sure. Our journey will suffer as a result. [3:16]

Activities for Your Group's Journey

1. Do you tend toward compulsively monitoring your progress or are you more likely to grow lax in this area? When you do, is your natural inclination toward evaluating doctrinal or practical issues?

2. What spiritual practices give you the sense of being closest to God? (Some examples might include prayer, Bible reading, journaling, singing, or practical acts of service.) As you hear the other members of the group respond to this question, is there a spiritual practice that you need to restart? Something that you could try for the first time?

3. What is one especially striking example of how God has shown his trustworthiness in your life? How has this helped you hold on to your end of the rope?

4. In addition to conversation, what are some other ways we can spur one another on toward love and good deeds? What is hard about this responsibility? How can your small group improve in this area? Pray as a group that God will give you the ability and the willingness to develop into this type of community.

5. What can we do to prepare ourselves for receiving such "spurring" with a teachable and humble attitude?

And let us consider how we may spur one another on toward love and good deeds. ^{25}Let us not give up meeting together, as some are in the habit of doing, but let us encourage one another—and all the more as you see the Day approaching.

CHAPTER TEN

CONFIDENCE FOR THE JOURNEY

HEBREWS 11:1-40

The clarity of your sight determines the confidence of your steps. Those of you who wear glasses or contacts know exactly what I mean. In fact, I was reminded only a few nights ago myself. Not making adequate progress on this book, I decided to work late and get up early. Not wanting to disturb my family, I decided to just sleep for a couple of hours in my office. Not considering the implications, I decided to take off my glasses. Not having a brain, I paid no attention to where I placed them. Bad idea. I can't read the top letter on an eye chart without them.

When the alarm clock went off, the comedy routine ensued. Grumbling at my stupidity (but grateful for my solitude), I began crawling and feeling my way around the room. Every movement was tentative. I had to feel the carpet in front of me before I crawled on it (crushed glasses = no driving capacity). My hands had to move across the desk tentatively, because I couldn't see what I was on the verge of knocking off. I had placed the glasses in an unusual location (the keyboard tray which slides underneath my desk). As a result, conservative estimates are that it took four minutes to find them. These were, without question, the most tentative moments of the day. They may well have been some of the most tentative moments of my life. Once I could see, crawling gave way to confidence.

The same is true for us spiritually. Hebrews 11 contains perhaps the most familiar material in the entire book. It is essentially a biographical sermon on Habakkuk 2:3-4 (as cited in Heb 10:37-38). What does it mean to be a person who lives by faith? According to this chapter it means seeing life through a new set of lenses (11:1, 2, 7, 10, 13, 14). It means recognizing that the invaluable is often invisible. It means living with courageous, active trust. It means obeying God, whose voice can be heard even though his face cannot be seen.

> Living by faith means recognizing
> that the invaluable is often invisible.

When it comes to biblical models of such faith, Abraham stands front and center. No biblical figure is mentioned more frequently in relationship to faith, and he is highlighted here in Hebrews 11 as well. He was far from perfect (take a look at Gen 12:10ff, for example). His life admittedly shows that God does not transform our sight through foolproof corrective eye surgery. His life is also reflective, however, of the positive summary statement found in 11:13-16. These verses may apply to the rest of the folks in the chapter, but they are presented as an interlude in the story of Abraham. Therefore, let's take a closer look at his life as representative of the entire chapter's message.

Travel Confidently:
Even When God's Promise Seems Vague (11:8)

Hebrews begins where Abraham's direct encounters with God began. The specific message Abraham hears from God is, "It is time to take a trip." This is a pivotal, unprecedented moment; and, it happened to a guy who had rampant idolatry in his family and personal history (Josh 24:2).

Imagine Abraham's explanation to his wife. If Sarah asked why they were moving the only answer he could give was "God told me to." If Sarah asked where they were moving, his only honest response would have been "I don't know." We tend to assume that God revealed everything to Abraham up front. In reality, Genesis 12:1, 7 appear to indicate that God didn't tell Abraham where he was going until he arrived. (Genesis 11:31 and 12:5 are given from the perspective of the "narrator," not Abraham). "Destination Unknown" is fine for youth group, but it is a little tough when your whole life is at stake.

Departing would have been no small thing either. It required leaving the realm of the familiar and secure. Ur was ideally located near the Euphrates river, in what we have come to know as the "Fertile Crescent." Scholars estimate the city's population was between

300,000 and 400,000 at the time of Abraham—largely because the alternatives were not appealing. This isn't exactly the kind of situation that makes a person anxious to call 1-800-GO-RYDER. Then again, it is also hard to reserve a moving van when you don't know where you are going. What causes a person like this to embark on a journey like this? The right set of glasses makes a difference.

Do you need to know all of the details regarding your life journey before you are ready to take the first step? I work at a college; therefore, I spend a lot of time around people who are consumed with figuring out their future. Then I engage in hallway conversations after Sunday worship and realize how focused folks are on the future. Home group snack time and prayer time evidences more of the same. All of these conversations are more than a window into the souls of others—they are a mirror reflecting my own.

> **God wants me to be his person *today*.**

Therefore, we need to wrestle with a fundamental issue illustrated from the life of Abraham. God wants me to be his person *today*. He wants me to take *this* step confidently, trustingly, and obediently. God's voice ultimately only seems vague, because our final destination is not an unknown (Heb 11:13-16). The meantime matters, but sometimes God reveals things step by step.

Travel Confidently:
Even When God's Promise Seems Distant (11: 9-10)

Abraham's faith journey did not end once he entered Canaan. In many ways, the trip was only beginning. Though Abraham now knew his destination, he had to face a gnawing reality. God's promises, though true, are often delivered on a timetable different from that which we would prefer.

84

✝

> **God's promises, though true, are often delivered on a different timetable.**

Two primary issues in Abraham's life illustrate this fact. The first challenge involved the land which Abraham's descendants had been promised. You see, that is precisely the point. The land had been promised to Abraham's offspring (12:7). Yet, since the promise was made to Abraham, there is a sense in which the promise was for him. It just wasn't something he fully experienced in his own lifetime. Abraham died before his offspring possessed the land. While in the land that would someday belong to those wearing his name, his life consisted of putting in and pulling out tent pegs. Not exactly the most settled life, and it was the kind of existence that could make one long for the good old days in Ur. Oh, he possessed a little sliver of land in Canaan. It's just that the land he held was the burial plot in which he and Sarah were buried and he had to pay for that! (Genesis 23)

> **Abraham didn't long for home.**
> **Instead he longed for Home.**

According to Hebrews 11:14-16, however, Abraham didn't long for home. Instead he longed for Home, the ultimate destination of his journey; a relationship with God that transcends latitude and longitude. Abraham saw by faith the fulfillment of God's promise regarding Canaan, even though he never physically observed it. Because of that faith, he also received a permanent address in the New Jerusalem.

The second challenge occurs between the lines of Hebrews 11:10-11, and involves the promise of a son. The land had been promised to Abraham's descendants, yet he had no children. In Genesis 15, God had promised Abraham (then named Abram) that the promised son would come from his own body. Later, in Genesis 17, God had reinforced this promise and changed his name to Abraham. Both names have meanings that relate to the same core idea—fatherhood. Every time Abraham heard his name, he was reminded that the promise of God had not yet been fulfilled. Abraham departed Ur at age 75. The next 24 years were spent wondering when God would give him a son. How could he be the father of many people when he wasn't the father of any people?

This issue was more difficult for Abraham's family to wait out. Genesis 16 records Abraham's obtaining of a son, Ishmael, through a union with his wife's servant. It reflects an effort on the part of the family to obtain God's promised blessing through their own efforts. While it was Sarah's idea, Abraham was clearly an active participant. As a result he has a son, but not the child through which the promise would be brought to fulfillment. In Abraham's defense, the promise recorded in Genesis 15:4 indicated the child would come from his body, not necessarily as a result of a union with Sarah. On the other hand, Abraham should probably have known better. Even this great patriarch struggled with the distance between God's spoken promise and God's fulfilled promise.

What about you? Do you have to see the fulfillment of all God's promises with your own eyes before you will trust his words, his will, and his ways? Can you see the fulfillment of those promises, even while they remain unseen? I'm not talking about simply a visualization exercise or a vague optimism. I'm talking about the fact that, insofar as it depends on God, a promise made is a promise kept. Can you walk as confidently in the land of "promise made" as you would in the land of "promise kept"?

> Can you walk as confidently in the land of "promise made" as you would in the land of "promise kept"?

Walk Confidently:
Even When God's Promise Seems Impossibly Good (11:11)

Finally Abraham got the word. The time had come for Sarah to shop for maternity clothing and start stocking up on diapers. They could finally discuss where to put the nursery and look for birth announcements. There's only one problem, and both Genesis 18:11 and Hebrews 11:11 highlight it. Both Mom and Dad were too old for this. They were not just too old to handle it emotionally; they were too old to handle it physically. They did want a son, mind you. It just seemed like a biological impossibility. The fundamental question, however, is highlighted in Genesis 18:14 where Abraham was asked, "Is anything too hard for the Lord?"

According to Paul, Abraham's response was to believe God (Rom 4:19-21). Abraham had once laughed to himself at his promise (Gen 17:17), but his giggle was one of faith. Sarah laughed as well (Gen 18:12), but hers was apparently one of doubt. God's response was essentially as follows: "Since everyone seems to think it is so funny, just name the kid Laughter" (the Hebrew meaning of Isaac).

> When the promises of God seem too good to be true, what do you do?

When the promises of God seem too good to be true, what do you do? Women do not typically carry around birth control pills and Geritol in the same purse. Anyone who has passed seventh grade health knows that if you need one, you don't need the other. The question still remains, however. Is anything too difficult for God?

It is important for Christians to guard themselves against a vending machine theology. There is a reason why believers don't sing Disney's "When You Wish Upon a Star" at baptism services. It isn't God's responsibility to make our every dream come true. On the other hand, it is easy to slide into a curmudgeon Christianity that assumes God isn't behind the improbable-but-good events of life. This is equally unbiblical (Jas 1:17). Maintaining balance requires more than good equilibrium; it requires good eyesight.

> It isn't God's responsibility to make
> our every dream come true.

Travel Confidently:
Even When God's Promise Seems Confusing (11:17-19)

The portrait of Abraham's faith reached its apex when Abraham reached Moriah. Most sermons and lessons from Genesis 22 wax eloquent regarding the emotional stress that Abraham must surely have felt as he made this most difficult three-day journey. From a parent's perspective, it is virtually impossible to imagine the overwhelming burden such a command would create. Interestingly, however, neither Genesis 22 nor Hebrews 11 emphasize this emotional element. It is not because the biblical writers are cautious about presenting him as emotionally distraught. In fact, Abraham is presented as deeply burdened over having to give up a son (Gen 21:11). The child in that case was Ishmael (the son born to Sarah's servant), not Isaac (the son born to Sarah). This is not to suggest Abraham was detached and disinterested in Genesis 22, but to clarify the primary dilemma in the text.

Abraham's perplexing problem requires harmonizing the two commands of God. On the one hand, God had promised Abraham many offspring through Isaac. On the other hand, God had commanded the father to kill the son. Abraham knew both messages were from God, but how could both be true? What does a person of faith do when the voice of God doesn't seem to make sense?

> In an amazing display of faith, he reasoned
> that God was God enough to achieve his promise
> without contradicting his command.

Here's what Abraham did. In an amazing display of faith, he reasoned that God was God enough to achieve his promise without contradicting his command. With no historical precedent to draw upon, he decided that God would vindicate his obedience by raising his son back to life. This would enable Abraham to obey God by killing his son and yet receive offspring through that same son. As he raised the knife, Abraham had given up his boy for dead. This is why Hebrews says that, figuratively speaking, Isaac was raised to life. God gave the father his son back.

What an example of ferocious faith! How do you respond when the voice of God seems confusing? Many people use their minds to think of every possible reason why God's Word cannot be consistent in and authoritative for our lives. Others use their best reasoning powers to think of every possible reason why God can be both believed and trusted. The decision is not primarily determined by how clearly one thinks; it is determined by how clearly one sees, not with outer eyes, but with the heart.

> **This would be a good time to make the Great Physician your optometrist.**

Therefore, this would be a good time to make the Great Physician your optometrist. Abraham and a host of others from Hebrews 11 are willing to testify regarding the difference he can make. Allow him to do what only he can accomplish. Doing so will improve both the quality of your sight and the quality of your journey. 🔲

Activities for Your Group's Journey

1. Is there an area of concern regarding your future that is keeping you from focusing on being God's man or woman today?

2. Have you ever been through a situation where the path on which God was leading you seemed vague at the time? Has He provided clarity regarding the situation yet? If so, how did he do so? What helped you remain faithful in the meantime? Use this as an opportunity to allow your experience to encourage the rest of the group.

3. Is there an area in which God is currently challenging you to venture out from the familiar and/or secure? If appropriate, share this with the group and ask the group to pray for you in this regard. If not, find a prayer partner with whom you can share.

4. Describe a situation in which you had to choose whether to invest your mind in trusting God's truth or doubting it. Are there areas of Scripture that currently seem to you as if they contradict? Perhaps this would be a good time to get perspective from other group members on the issue. If not, seek the counsel of someone you respect regarding the issue.

5. Who is someone whose faith has been especially exemplary and encouraging to you? If they are alive, write them a note specifically explaining how they have made a difference in your life. If they are deceased, write God a thank you note regarding how He used them in your life.

Memory Verse
Hebrews 11:1-2

Now faith is being sure of what we hope for and certain of what we do not see. ²This is what the ancients were commended for.

CHAPTER ELEVEN

RESOLVE FOR THE JOURNEY

HEBREWS 12:1-13

Have you ever been on a journey that seemed like it would never end? A long, hard trip can take away your desire to go back or go on.

John Colter has gone down in American history as one of the greatest explorers and trappers of the early 1800s. He was, for example, the first Caucasian to see the territory that is now Yellowstone National Park. He was one of only ten men on the Lewis and Clark expedition chosen to make the final ten mile hike to the Pacific Ocean. He has also gone down in history as one of America's greatest runners, even though he never set foot on a track. He is famous for a single race—the one of and for his life.

Colter had been trapping with a friend in Blackfeet territory. While canoeing down a stretch of Montana river, they heard some rustling along the riverbank. Colter was soon the primary focus of a pow-wow. His friend was killed attempting to escape; now John's fate was being decided. He had killed Blackfeet on two previous trapping expeditions and was, therefore, an especially desirable catch. The original plan was to use him for target practice, but he ended up as prey in a "human hunt." Though details vary according to the source, the trapper was stripped and given a 500-yard head start.

Ahead of Colter was six miles of sagebrush, cactus, and sharp stones. His feet were immediately sliced open and embedded with thorns, but the trapper-turned-racer continued to focus on a distant cluster of trees. By the three-mile mark, only a handful remained in the hunt. John was on the verge of being caught at four miles, but he fought off the brave who reached him. Though running had stressed his body to the point that blood was flowing from his nose and mouth, Colter made it to a river marked by the cluster of trees.

John dove into the icy water and hid under a driftwood raft that was caught at the edge of a sandbar. The Indians swarmed the river and even stood on the raft itself, but didn't find him. Under the cover of darkness, he finally began the trip toward Bighorn (the closest trading post). It was 150 miles away. Stripped of everything but his resolve, the half-frozen and half-delirious trapper embarked on the seven-day journey to safe land and legendary status. His name has been subsequently attached to a song in the film *Westward Ho*, a building at Disneyland, and a town in Wyoming.

The kicker, though, is the part left out of most accounts. When Colter had adequately recovered, he returned to get his traps! Again, he was attacked. Again, he managed to escape unharmed. Incredibly, this man led another trapping expedition to the same place. Again, his party was attacked. Again, he managed to escape (though five in his group were killed). Finally, even John Colter decided enough was enough. He quit trapping and adopted the quieter life of a farmer.

Life is kind of like that, isn't it? The Christian journey can be tiring, painful, perplexing, exasperating, and just downright long. At times, the hassles are our own fault. On other occasions, we are relatively innocent bystanders who somehow get caught in the fray. Sometimes, the hardships we face are directly, strategically, and intentionally planned.

> The Christian journey can be tiring, painful, perplexing, exasperating, and just downright long. Such experiences push us in one of two directions: success or surrender.

Source notwithstanding, such experiences push us in one of two directions: success or surrender. Adversity galvanizes the determination of some folks. Others are disillusioned by difficulty. Some, like John Colter, start with almost superhuman resolve and eventually get worn down. Hunting is less fun when you get on the wrong end of the expedition. In Colter's case, it seems the pursuers who never caught him physically eventually wore him down mentally. The same can happen to you and me.

You can especially get worn down when you are facing hardship particularly and primarily because you are on the Christian pilgrimage. Work environments can often be brutal, but the frustration is especially intense when someone is stabbing you in the back because you lead a break room Bible study. Family reunions can test anyone's confidence in God's goodness, but it is especially exasperating when siblings roll their eyes instead of closing their eyes as you pray for the meal. Marriage causes consternation to many, but an unbelieving spouse can turn the back deck into a boxing ring. Friendships are often fragile, but when they shatter due to value conflicts, more than just a relationship is often fractured.

> We are challenged to allow such circumstances to strengthen rather than suffocate our commitment.

Hebrews 12 is provided to hearten believers against an onslaught of persecutions and problems. We are challenged to allow such circumstances to strengthen rather than suffocate our commitment. The folks who first received this material faced significant pressures. Their Jewish neighbors wanted to know why the faith that was sufficient for 1500 years of Israel's history was suddenly not good enough. Their governmental officials would soon begin a more systematic persecution of Christians in the region. For the sake of their present and future resolve, they needed a strengthening word from God. I've got a hunch we can use one as well.

These verses especially call us to staying power through repetition of the word *perseverance*. It is used three times, even though it is translated *endure* in verses two and three). Such rugged resilience is the opposite of *shrinking back* (10:38). This latter term was sometimes used to describe an athlete who grew weary of the race and decided to quit the contest. Here we are challenged to finish rather than forfeit. In order to help keep us from giving up, the writer of Hebrews gives us three words of guidance.

Look Around (v. 1)

We are first encouraged to focus on the examples of those who have preceded us. The specific examples in view are those in Hebrews 11 who were able to stand firmly by faith even though they lived prior to the coming of Jesus. The picture is that of an athletic arena with the Old Testament faithful in the stands. These witnesses, however, are more than spectators. Whenever used in the Bible, this word involves actively testifying about something—either with one's lips or one's life. Here, they bear testimony to the truth of Habakkuk 2:3-4 (Heb 10:38). God testified on their behalf (11:2), now they are testifying on his. Their example honors God and helps us. It is much easier to finish a race when you know someone has successfully completed the course before you.

92

‡

C
H
A
P
T
E
R

For years, running a sub-four-minute mile was considered impossible. Physiologists thought the mind would actually rebel against the strain and the body would shut down. One expert dared suggest the possibility of success, but thought it could happen only if the runner passed out precisely at the finish line. On an overcast day in March 1954, Roger Bannister defeated competitors and skeptics alike. Ironically he did so at Oxford University (what an appropriate place to confound the experts!). Bannister understood the implications of 3:59.4 better than anyone. When interviewed afterward, he said, "*après moi le déluge.*" My French isn't very good, but the basic idea is, "now that I have broken this mental and physical barrier that all you experts deemed an insurmountable obstacle, watch out because a whole lot of others are going to do it as well." He was not just a good runner; he was a good prognosticator. Within two years over fifty people had run a sub-four-minute mile.

There is a sense in which these witnesses do the same for us. They have already completed the race. The issue isn't so much that they are gazing upon us, but rather that we can look at them. As people of God they show us that it can be done and how it can be done. They weren't more innately gifted for the race than we are. The writer of Hebrews indicates that if anyone has an advantage, it is those who live in the afterglow of God's fullest self-revelation in Jesus. They weren't necessarily better people than we are. Most of them had main points in their personal testimonies that would make us blush. We tend to view these folks as superheroes; when we do, we miss God's intent for the text. He isn't saying we can't be like them, he's saying we can!

These days are our moment on the stage of human history. This is our opportunity to become part of a glorious heritage. The relentless pursuit of God's approval often means we will do poorly in the court of public opinion. So did they. We are sometimes viewed as oddballs. So were they. God's estimate of such folk? The world is not worthy of them (11:38). When tempted to lose heart and give up the race, remember whose approval matters most.

93

‡

C
H
A
P
T
E
R

Resolve for the Journey 11

Look Within (v. 1)

The second word of counsel is to carefully scrutinize our own spiritual condition. Runners prosper by traveling light, so they are compulsive about calories and agonize over aerodynamics. It has always been so. If you recall from history or art class, Greek athletes didn't get many endorsement contracts from the fashion industry. There wasn't anywhere to sew the patch! Athletes are vigilant because success is not just determined by what you put on, but also by what you take off. The same concept applies to our race of faith. The fact that our burdens are spiritual rather than physical makes their removal even more important.

The items that hinder are not specifically distinguished from those that entangle (v. 1). Rather than talking about two separate categories, the writer is reinforcing one basic idea. We need to fully partner with the Holy Spirit in removing the burden of sin from our lives so we will be free to run our best. Doing so demands a ferocious commitment to ongoing reflection and reevaluation.

Here's why. It is amazingly easy to accumulate extra baggage. In fact we accumulate extra weight spiritually in the same ways we do physically. Sometimes, it happens as a result of inattention. We just wake up one morning and realize, "I've really made it more difficult for myself to run the race!" Regular reflection is the spiritual equivalent of stepping on the scales each morning. On other occasions, we are somewhat conscious of the process and simply fail to address the issue. We know we are carrying an extra burden, but avoid dealing with the issue until we simply get sick of running that way. Regular reorientation helps us avoid delaying the inevitable.

> Regular reflection is the spiritual equivalent of stepping on the scales each morning.

Simply put, Christian runners need a relentless commitment to traveling light. Such determination will seem fanatical in the eyes of many. Just like a focused athlete, however, we must show a healthy disinterest in such assessments. Champions don't become champions by following the crowd.

Look Up (vv. 2-3)

If we want to finish well, however, we must not become entirely self-absorbed. Similarly, we cannot merely focus on our predecessors or our peers. Jesus is the ultimate model of what it means to run faithfully and fearlessly for God. Looking to Jesus, however, is not like gazing at a piece of sentimental sports memorabilia. We are not to simply look at him, but rather to look to him. The emphasis in this section is that Jesus endured a more difficult path than we have, yet he persevered. Two specific areas of Jesus' example are highlighted here.

First, Jesus kept the finish line in view (12:2). The terms *author* and *perfecter* essentially mean that Jesus both started and finished the process necessary to bring us salvation. Jesus found great joy in completing that mission, even though it included physical suffering and cultural shame. For Jews, crucifixion was shameful because it showed the sufferer was under God's curse (Deut 21:23). Romans reserved crucifixion for common criminals that were not Roman citizens. In an ironic wordplay, however, verse 2 notes that Jesus scorned the scorning he received. For those hours of torture, He was unashamed to be treated shamefully. This was not because his suffering was somehow watered down. Rather, the goal was more important to Jesus than the difficulty of getting there.

> **Jesus both started and finished the process necessary to bring us salvation.**

Second, the mistreatment was at the hands of sinful people (12:3). Sometimes we get the impression that all suffering is somehow our fault. The example of Jesus shows, however, that those who belong to God do sometimes suffer innocently. There is a certain risk that comes with being identified as a person belonging to God. Sometimes a person that is mad at God will take it out on us. Sometimes one who doesn't accurately understand God will mistreat us in the name of God. Jesus experienced this, so those who wear his name should not be surprised when the same happens to them (Matt 10:11ff).

Herein lies the significance of Hebrews 12:4-11 within the overall section. Suffering for Christ causes some people to question God, but it causes others to question themselves. "If I were really God's child," one might think, "I wouldn't have to deal with this." Proverbs 3 occurs in a series of proverbs addressed from a father to a son. As both Proverbs 3:11-12 and the example of Jesus demonstrate, suffering for the faith is not evidence one is outside the family. It is evidence one is inside the family. Our resolve is strengthened when we recognize God is actually affirming us through affliction.

> **Suffering is not evidence one is outside the family; it is evidence one is inside the family.**

Furthermore, God is big enough to use the mistreatment of his children in positive ways (12:9-11). Jesus' crucifixion was the most undeserved moment of suffering in history. God made it into the greatest victory in history. While our experiences pale in comparison to Jesus' (v. 4), God can similarly transform the treachery we experience into triumph. Like a mature human parent, God resists the urge to spare his children from difficult circumstances. Instead, he shapes his children into his likeness through times of trial.

> Jesus' crucifixion was the most
> undeserved moment of suffering in history.
> God made it into the greatest victory in history.

This recognition can help us finish strong. All runners know that a "no pain, no pain" philosophy sounds more appealing than "no pain, no gain." Committed athletes, however, recognize that pain is the pathway to victory. Therefore, they do everything within their power to strip off self-inflicted burdens, while simultaneously embracing external pressures that come. Similarly, we must remove the entanglements of sin while also embracing persecution as God's learning lab. By looking in the right directions, we can run with renewed perspective. Rather than losing heart and giving up (v. 5), our limbs can be strengthened and our path straightened (vv. 12-13).

Perhaps you are running at peak form right now. If so, don't allow your current condition to become a curse. As top-notch athletes realize, complacency can become one's greatest competitor. Maybe you are currently running adequately, but not exceptionally. If so, commit yourself to paying the price. Partner with the Holy Spirit so your full potential is realized. Then again, you might be really struggling right now. Perhaps all you can manage right now is a limp. If so, keep limping. God is pleased with people who can barely run but remain in the running. Limp until you can jog. Jog until you can run. Run until you can sprint. The goal is not to accumulate style points. This is a race, not a beauty pageant. Put one foot in front of the other until you see the end in sight.

I love the story of John Akhwari, the best-known last place finisher in Olympic track history. In the 1968 marathon, this gritty Tanzanian stumbled on the streets of Mexico City and suffered a significant knee injury. Nevertheless he continued the race. His efforts to compensate for the knee injury resulted in excruciating leg cramps. Still he kept running. "My head told me to quit," he would later say, "but my heart told me to keep going." Almost two hours after the event had been won, he finally reached the stadium for the concluding lap. Most of the crowd had long since departed, but the few hundred remaining spectators rose to their feet with thunderous applause. After crossing the finish line, Akhwari simply walked off the track. He didn't even acknowledge the cheering crowds, because he didn't want it to seem as if he had done something extraordinary. Incredulous interviewers asked him why he had continued the race under such daunting and potentially defeating circumstances. The Tanzanian replied, "My country did not send me 7,000 miles to start a race. They sent me 7,000 miles to finish it."

As citizens of an enduring, unshakable kingdom (12:28), the same is true for you and me. Let's finish with a flourish, if we can. If not, let's finish the best we can. This race is far too important to quit. 3:16

Activities for Your Group's Journey

1. It is time for some brutally honest assessment regarding your current condition. Are you limping, jogging, or running well?

2. Spend significant time this week praying for God to help you see the primary hindrances that are currently slowing you down. Make a list of the most pressing issues and develop a practical action plan to deal with them. Please understand—we don't overcome entanglements simply by our own willpower. This list is a means by which we can partner with God to run our best. Share one issue and corresponding action plan with the group. Find a person in your group who will hold you accountable for your action plan, and do the same for them.

3. What are the advantages of looking to examples of those who have already completed the race? Are there any potential disadvantages that come with doing so? How does focusing on Jesus help us keep other examples in perspective?

4. Has there been a recent circumstance in which you have experienced hardship specifically due to your Christian faith? If so, what lessons has God taught you through the learning lab of suffering? How have those experiences and lessons encouraged you? How have they enabled you to be a source of strength for others?

5. Focus your prayer time on those within the group who are currently limping. If group members are all doing well, pray for people outside the group who are struggling in the journey right now.

Memory Verse Hebrews 12:2-3

Let us fix our eyes on Jesus, the author and perfecter of our faith, who for the joy set before him endured the cross, scorning its shame, and sat down at the right hand of the throne of God. ³Consider him who endured such opposition from sinful men, so that you will not grow weary and lose heart.

CHAPTER TWELVE

REMINDERS FOR THE JOURNEY

HEBREWS 13:1-25

I have a memory shortage. If only I were like my computer, so that the memory deficiency could be solved by a mail order catalog. Since my problem is not so easily solved, I sometimes find myself getting into trouble. Especially when I forget something important on a trip. Perhaps you have also noticed that the quality of a journey is directly impacted by what you remember (or forget) to bring along with you.

Take, for example, the Christmas of 1993. We were living in central Illinois at the time, and the church we served had a Christmas Eve communion service. My parents and in-laws lived in a town about 3½ hours away, so my wife and our children had headed there for an extended holiday visit. I had stayed behind to help with the Christmas Eve service and was planning to join them late that evening. My only responsibility was to make sure that I remembered the Christmas presents.

I arrived at the home of my in-laws later that evening. My wife Francene was amazed at how quickly I was able to unload the car. I was much less surprised, since all I had to unload was my travel bag. It didn't even hit me until she asked, "Where are the presents?" Have you ever had that feeling? It defies simple definition or description, but if you have ever had it, you know exactly what I mean. It is that feeling you get in your stomach when you know you have committed the stupidest act in your personal (and perhaps all of human) history. It is that sudden awareness that you have made your biggest life blunder in the one place where all of your relatives are present (no pun intended) to relish the moment.

I tried to explain that the presents were hidden in an obscure location behind the tree. I waxed eloquent regarding the preoccupation of mind that is characteristic of all those involved with planning and executing a Christmas Eve service. I tried to divert everyone's attention by breaking into a chorus of "Oh Come All Ye Faithful." There was no hiding the truth, however. All the presents were over three hours away and a winter storm prohibited my return. No presents for our kids, our parents, our siblings, our nieces and nephews . . . none. Now we know that presents are peripheral to the true meaning of Christmas, and our family has worked hard to de-emphasize their significance in holiday celebrations. When you have two kids under the age of five, and there are no presents, however . . . well, it is not a pretty picture. One person's poor memory can mess up the trip for everyone.

The writer of Hebrews realized this, so he concludes his letter with a series of reminders. These are not truths people are hearing for the first time. Much effective preaching and teaching, however, is not primarily concerned with teaching people something new. It includes helping folks believe what they believe and reminding people of what they already know. Hebrews 13 addresses several such concerns and they provide an effective conclusion to our study. As we consider this chapter, two issues are crucial.

First, the memory problem these Christians are facing is not merely a mental struggle. While they may need to think more regularly about these issues, the problem is also practical. These folks are journeying through hostile territory. The pressure they face from both Jews and Romans is causing them to be tempted to neglect things they know they should be doing.

Second, the reminders in this chapter especially address community life within the family of faith. Difficult circumstances can vitally strengthen or virtually sever relationships. Early Christians especially needed one another, because many were subsequently disowned by friends and family. Family relationships are significant in any culture, but in the biblical world the loss was especially painful and significant. Christian brothers and sisters were the only family some of these folks had. Perhaps you know the feeling. The following commands are designed to help believers strengthen one another when the going gets tough.

> Difficult circumstances can vitally strengthen
> or virtually sever relationships.

Remember to Love Those in the Family

The command to continually love one another (v. 1) is an umbrella statement that helps us understand the whole chapter. All the following commands are essentially specific ways we can live out the responsibility reflected in this first one. The phrase "love as brothers" is a translation of a single Greek verb, from which we take the term Philadelphia. Sports fans are already aware of the irony of this, since the City of Brotherly Love has not always lived up to its name. Please understand that I want no part of perpetuating an inaccurate stereotype. I know there are wonderful people in Philadelphia and generalizations are dangerous. The reputation has been well earned, however. Here are some of the classic examples, courtesy of newspaper columnist Wes Allison:

(1) Santa Claus was once pelted with snowballs during a halftime show.

(2) Their own cheerleaders have been pelted with snowballs.

(3) Fights in the stands are routine.

(4) Veterans Stadium even has had its own jail and magistrate's court, so that arrested fans can be adjudicated without leaving the building.

(5) Children were booed during a recent Punt, Pass, and Kick competition.[1]

The reputation extends beyond the realm of athletics. Santa Claus was also booed during the Mother's Day parade one year; and, when legendary high-wire walker Karl Wallenda attempted to traverse Veteran's stadium, some observers threw debris at him![2] Perhaps Santa Claus deserves ridicule for showing up seven months early, but what about poor Karl Wallenda? Maybe these folks need to remember who they are and where they live.

Hebrews reminds us of a more painful and tragic potential irony. Christians are called brothers at strategic places in the letter (3:1, 12; 10:19); now, we are challenged to live up to this designation in our care for one another. Failure to do so makes a mockery of our family name.

At first glance it would seem we live out this command by having warm feelings toward one another. "Love" in this context is not primarily an emotion, contrary to popular perceptions of the term. Rather, it communicates the idea of relentless covenant commitment that is actively demonstrated in everyday life. Since family relationship is an ongoing reality, the tangible evidence of family commitment should be consistently evident as well.

Remember the Travelers in the Family

The first specific command involves demonstrating hospitality to those in need. Verse one shows such kindness is especially to be shown toward those who belong to God, even if they aren't known by us (v. 2I). Doing so enables us to join the heritage of the hospitable, of which Abraham stood as the ultimate Jewish example (Genesis 18 is alluded to in the last phrase of verse 2). There were several reasons why such ministry was important in the first-century world, even though inns were available. First, inns contained the risk of physical danger. Robberies were relatively common, and Plato even records an extreme instance in which an innkeeper took his customers hostage. Second, inns were places of spiritual danger. Immorality flourished there, to the point that one ancient writer compared innkeeping to running a brothel. Of course, not all inns were this bad, but the core issue is the human heart and not the environment. Those who frequently travel alone on business attest to the temptations that can surface when one is far from home and alone. Finally, hosting people provided an opportunity for the development of ongoing and enriching relationships with other believers.

The second and third issues are especially relevant today. It is common for traveling Christian workers to stay in hotels. This is not automatically bad, of course. When I travel, however, I often choose to stay in homes. This both prevents me from potential temptations and enables me to meet people I would not have otherwise known. The showing of hospitality on my journeys helps me on my ultimate journey.

Remember the Persecuted in the Family

The next reminder stressed by the author of Hebrews concerns the imprisoned. Although this verse is often used in support of prison ministry, it is especially those imprisoned for their faith that are in view (cf. Heb 10:32-34). This was a primary way early Christians could identify with persecuted brothers and sisters such as Timothy (13:23). The "remembering" called for here requires more than a memory magnet on the refrigerator. During the Roman empire, care for prisoners primarily took place according to the MCI plan—friends and family. Prisoners were dependent on loved ones to provide them with clothing and food. Those who had been disowned by their families when they came to Christ were especially dependent on their brothers and sisters in the faith. Even if we do not directly experience such treatment (cf. 12:1ff), we are to completely identify with those who do. We have a responsibility not to neglect our brothers and sisters in places like the Sudan,

Indonesia, and North Korea. When we suffer, the issue is hard to remove from the forefront of our minds. The sufferings of other Christians should impact us similarly. Remembering them includes prayer and, where possible, practical provision. We share a common journey and have an opportunity to make theirs a little easier.

> The "remembering" called for here requires more than a memory magnet on the refrigerator.

Remember to Keep Marital Commitments within the Family

The third major reminder addresses the importance of avoiding sexual immorality. Our theology of community must extend into the sphere of home relationships, including marriage. Indeed, an authentic theology of community begins here for those who are married. Adultery is a violation of one's marriage covenant, but if one's marriage partner and/or adultery partner are Christians, it is specifically a community violation against the church as well. While there are a number of helpful ways to affair-proof one's marriage, one of the most neglected is the active recognition that the impacted parties are brothers or sisters in Christ. When we demonstrate the continual love for one another reflected in verse one, we will be less likely to venture into the sphere of inappropriate relationships.

The twenty-first century church desperately needs to remember this teaching. Christians must deal proactively, directly, and redemptively with crossgender relationships in the family of faith. One of the greatest strengths of Christian community, relational intimacy, can become a tool used by our adversary to destroy relationships with God and others. For example, the powerful bonding that occurs in home group Bible studies has served as a catalyst to extramarital affairs between participants.

Remember to Develop Contentment within the Family

At first glance, there might not appear to be a significant connection between adultery and lack of material contentment. The two issues are frequently mentioned side by side in the New Testament, however (1 Cor 5:11; Eph 4:18; 1 Thess 4:3-6). At the core, both sins reveal both a selfish spirit and a deep lack of contentment with God's provision in one's life. The antidote to this poison is a deep awareness of God's presence, provision, and protection (Ps 118:6-7).

Hebrews 10:32-34 reminds us that these believers had once seen worse days materially and better days spiritually. At that time, they were willing to lose their possessions, if necessary, for the sake of standing firmly for Christ. Early Christians periodically faced great economic pressure when they held firmly for Christ. They were sometimes shut out of trade guilds (the ancient equivalent of trade unions) because of their refusal to practice idolatry. Those with businesses faced the temptation to hide their Christianity for the sake of economic prosperity. Those standing firmly for the cause of Christ faced the possibility of having their possessions taken, just as the emperor Claudius ordered in his persecution of these believers in 49 A.D. (this is the apparent background behind Heb 10:32-34).

It is easier to meet a need when we are free from greed.

On a more positive note, financial contentment also frees us to invest our resources in the well-being of others. It is easier to meet a need when we are free from greed. Such actions are ways we can offer a sacrifice of praise to the One who sacrificed his Son. On the back of U.S. currency is printed the phrase "In God We Trust." Our responsibility as Christians is to make that statement a reality rather than a cruel irony (vv. 5-6).

Remember to Respect Leaders within the Family

There are two primary sections of chapter thirteen that address the relationship between overseers and the rest of the community (vv. 7-8, 17). There are several implied lessons for leaders to understand and obey. The central thrust of the passage, however, addresses the responsibilities of those who are receiving oversight. Therefore, those responsibilities are our focus.

The first responsibility is to follow their example of faithfulness. Certainly this teaching implies that leaders should live exemplary lives. The leaders these Christians were called to remember had modeled healthy teaching and mature living. Of course, no human leader is perfect—this is why the writer of Hebrews highlights the consistency of Jesus in 13:8 (also see 13:20). Our primary orientation is toward the example of Jesus, but there is also great value in having someone to fol-

104
‡

C
H
A
P
T
E
R

low who is following Christ (1 Cor 11:1). The solution to a world full of imitation Christianity is Christianity worthy of being imitated. Godly examples are not only to be celebrated, they are to be copied (though not cloned).

> **The solution to a world full of imitation Christianity is Christianity worthy of being imitated.**

The second responsibility is to be the kind of follower who lightens a leader's load. Leaders are certainly accountable to God for how they function (v. 17). The term "watch over" probably relates particularly to the leader's responsibility for the doctrinal well-being of the congregation (1 Thess 5:12; 1 Tim 5:17; Jas 3:1), but no leadership task is insignificant to or unknown by God. Such a burden is heavy enough without the followers coming along and adding additional weight! The same God who watches leaders lead also observes how followers follow. Effectively fulfilling our various roles honors God and strengthens the family. Failing to do so is of no advantage to anyone except Satan since ministry is hamstrung in the process.

> **The same God who watches leaders lead also observes how followers follow.**

Small groups can be either a bane or a blessing in this regard. Disgruntled and discouraged believers can be reoriented, refueled, and refocused through the gift of community. By the same token, an unteachable and unsubmissive spirit can also prove to be a communicable disease! Our responsibility is not to remove the weight of the leader's mantle, but to make sure that the burden is God-given.

Remember the Head of the Family

Many communion tables are branded with some of the most familiar words spoken by Jesus: "Do this is remembrance of me." This book which is so focused on the supremacy of Jesus' person and work does not leave its primary theme untouched in its final chapter (Heb 13:9-15, 20-21). This focus provides the ultimate motivation to our memories. Perhaps the words etched into our family furniture should be etched into our hearts. "Do this in remembrance of me" can become the mission statement of our lives. When we find it hard to love a Christian brother or sister, hear our brother Jesus say, "Do this in remembrance of me." When hospitality is hard, hear One who lacked a home say, "Do this in remembrance of me." When it is hard to be content with a bed-partner or bank account, hear our Provider and the church's bridegroom say, "Do this in remembrance of me." When following the leaders is far from a game, hear the great Shepherd of the sheep say, "Do this in remembrance of me."

"Do this in remembrance of me" can become the mission statement of our lives.

What happens if we do? Everyone experiences a more graceful journey (13:22). ✠

---

[1] Wes Allison, "Fanatical Philly Fans Frighten Floridians," *St. Petersburg Times* (January 16, 2003).

[2] Rick Dean, "It's Not Always Easy to Love Our Brothers in Philly," *Topeka Capital-Journal* (Sept 27, 1998).

Activities for Your Group's Journey

1. What are some practical ways you or your group can minister to the Christian persecuted? See the College Press website (www.collegepress.com) for resources that can assist you in prayerful and practical support. Also see the website for recent experiences of persecuted believers. Consider adopting a group of persecuted believers as a group project.

2. Is it difficult for you to practice the ministry of hospitality? If so, what elements of our culture make it difficult for you/us to do so? Do you think God is pleased with our more detached forms of hospitality (such as giving money), or do you think he desires more direct involvement from Christians? Why? Should this involvement include opening our homes? What are the risks and blessings of doing so?

3. What are some things your group can do to protect against inappropriate male/female relationships? On the other hand, how do we avoid becoming so sensitive toward this issue that the legitimate beauty and diversity of Christian community ends up marred? Where are the biblical boundaries on this issue and to what extent is this a matter of Christian freedom?

4. Who is a leader in your church that you respect? Why? Perhaps this would be a good time to share with one another regarding the qualities in one another that you find worthy of imitation.

5. Are there God-given limitations to the submission a believer should show toward a church leader? What should Christians do in situations where they cannot submit to a leader in clear conscience?

6. What is the single greatest way that studying Hebrews has impacted your faith journey?

Memory Verse
Hebrews 13:20-21

May the God of peace, who through the blood of the eternal covenant brought back from the dead our Lord Jesus, that great Shepherd of the sheep, ²¹equip you with everything good for doing his will, and may he work in us what is pleasing to him, through Jesus Christ, to whom be glory for ever and ever. Amen.

About the Author

Dr. Jeff Snell is a professor at Ozark Christian College where he has taught since 1997. He has taught classes on the book of Hebrews as well as Expository Preaching, Issues in Interpretation, Homiletics, Old Testament History, and Doctrine of the End Times.

Jeff received his D.Min. from Southern Baptist Theological Seminary in 2002. He holds a M.Div. and a M.A. from Lincoln Christian Seminary and earned his B.Th. and B.B.L. from Ozark Christian College. He is a member of the Academy of Homiletics and the Evangelical Homiletics Society.

Jeff enjoys reading and sports. He and his wife Francene have been married since 1989 and have three children, Allisan, Andrew, and Antonia.